# THE WALL OF LIGHT

# THE WALL OF LIGHT

## NIKOLA TESLA
## AND THE X-12 SPACESHIP

By
Arthur H. Matthews, E.E.

ISBN-13: 978-1544107547
ISBN-10: 1544107544

PRINTING HISTORY
Matthews edition published 1971
Health Research edition published 1973
Saucerian Press edition published 1978
New Saucerian Press edition published 2017

Nikola Tesla

## Foreword

How did the world's greatest inventor invent? How did he carry out an invention? What sort of mentality did this wonder man have? Was his early life as commonplace as most boys'? What was the early training of this man from space? Was he an earth man? Did he come from the planet Venus? Was he born on a space ship? The answers to these and many other questions will be found in this story from the lips of the man himself.

In this autobiography concerning his early youth, and so on, we obtain a good insight into the wonderful life this man led. It reads like a fairy tale, but strange as it may be, it is true. Tesla was no common mortal. He led a charmed life--given up by doctors at least three times as dead, he was a young man at sixty and at seventy; with a brain just as keen the day he died, (if he did die, for many believe he did not). He always said he would live to the age of one hundred and fifty, so perhaps he is alive on Venus? That might be easy to believe now, for if man can build a rocket to the moon or Venus, there is no reason to doubt that science on that planet could be a thousand years ahead of earth man's. We know that space ships have landed on earth, all through the ages. Tesla said that he believed he came from the planet Venus, and during the landings of a space ship on my property, the members of that ship said that Tesla was a child from Venus. Tesla will tell you in his own words, what he believed. Read the story with care; there is a lot between the lines, as you will see. He had one great vice--his generosity. He could have been the richest man on earth. He made and spent millions. He was an idealist of the highest order, and to such men, money itself means but little.

Arthur Henry Matthews, E. E.

The progressive development of man is vitally dependent on invention. It is the most important product of his creative brain. Its ultimate purpose is the complete mastery of mind over the material world, the harnessing of the forces of nature to human needs. This is the difficult task of the inventor who is often misunderstood and unrewarded. But he finds ample compensation in the pleasing exercises of his powers and in the knowledge of being one of that exceptionally privileged class without whom the race would have long ago perished in the bitter struggle against pitiless elements. Speaking for myself, I have already had more than my full measure of this exquisite enjoyment; so much, that for many years my life was little short of continuous rapture. I am credited with being one of the hardest workers and perhaps I am, if thought is the equivalent of labour, for I have devoted to it almost all of my waking hours. But if work is interpreted to be a definite performance in a specified time according to a rigid rule, then I may be the worst of idlers.

Every effort under compulsion demands a sacrifice of life-energy. I never paid such a price. On the contrary, I have thrived on my thoughts. In attempting to give a connected and faithful account of my activities in this story of my life, I must dwell, however reluctantly, on the impressions of my youth and the circumstances and events which have been instrumental in determining my career. Our first endeavors are purely instinctive promptings of an imagination vivid and undisciplined. As we grow older reason asserts itself and we become more and more systematic and designing. But those early impulses, tho not immediately productive, are of the greatest moment and may shape our very destinies. Indeed, I feel now that had I understood and cultivated instead of supressing them, I would have added substantial value to my bequest to the world. But not until I had attained manhood did I realize that I was an inventor.

This was due to a number of causes. In the first place I had a brother who was gifted to an extraordinary degree; one of those rare phenomena of mentality which biological investigation has failed to explain. His premature death left my earth parents disconsolate. (I will explain my remark about my "earth parents" later.) We owned a horse which had been presented to us by a dear friend. It was a magnificent animal of Arabian breed, possessed of almost human intelligence, and was cared for and petted by the whole family, having on one occasion saved my father's life under remarkable circumstances.

My father had been called one winter night to perform an urgent duty and while crossing the mountains, infested by wolves, the horse became frightened and ran away, throwing him violently to the ground. It arrived home bleeding and exhausted, but after the alarm was sounded, immediately dashed off again, returning to the spot, and before the searching party were far on the way they were met by my father, who had recovered consciousness and remounted, not realizing that he had been lying in the snow for several hours. This horse was responsible for my brother's injuries from which he died. I witnessed the tragic scene and altho so many years have elapsed since, my visual impression of it has lost none of its force. The recollection of his attainments made every effort of mine seem dull in comparison. Anything I did that was creditable merely caused my parents to feel their loss more keenly. So I grew up with little confidence in myself.

But I was far from being considered a stupid boy, if I am to judge from an incident of which I have still a strong remembrance. One day the Aldermen were passing thru a street where I was playing with other boys. The oldest of these venerable gentlemen, a wealthy citizen, paused to give a silver piece to each of us. Coming to me, he suddenly stopped and commanded, "Look in my eyes." I met his gaze, my hand outstretched to receive the much valued coin, when to my dismay, he said, "No, not much; you can get nothing from me. You are too smart."

They used to tell a funny story about me. I had two old aunts with wrinkled faces, one of them having two teeth protruding like the tusks of an elephant, which she buried in my cheek every time she kissed me. Nothing would scare me more then the prospects of being by these affectionate, unattractive relatives. It happened that while being carried in my mother's arms, they asked me who was the prettier of the two. After examining their faces intently, I answered thoughtfully, pointing to one of them, "This here is not as ugly as the other."

Then again, I was intended from my very birth, for the clerical profession and this thought constantly oppressed me. I longed to be an engineer, but my father was inflexible. He was the son of an officer who served in the army of the Great Napoleon and in common with his brother, professor of mathematics in a prominent institution, had received a military education; but, singularly enough, later embraced the clergy in which vocation he achieved eminence. He was a very erudite man, a veritable natural philosopher, poet and writer and his sermons were said to be as eloquent as those of Abraham a-Sancta-Clara. He had a prodigious memory and frequently recited at length from works in several languages. He often remarked playfully that if some of the classics were lost he could restore them. His style of writing was much admired. He penned sentences short and terse and was full of wit and satire. The humorous remarks he made were always peculiar and characteristic. Just to illustrate, I may mention one or two instances.

Among the help, there was a cross-eyed man called Mane, employed to do work around the farm. He was chopping wood one day. As he swung the axe, my father, who stood nearby and felt very uncomfortable, cautioned him, "For God's sake, Mane, do not strike at what you are looking but at what you intend to hit."

On another occasion he was taking out for a drive, a friend who carelessly permitted his costly fur coat to rub on the carriage wheel. My father reminded him of it saying, "Pull in your coat; you are ruining my tire."

He had the odd habit of talking to himself and would often carry on an animated conversation and indulge in heated argument, changing the tone of his voice. A casual listener might have sworn that several people were in the room.

Altho I must trace to my mother's influence whatever inventiveness I possess, the training he gave me must have been helpful. It comprised all sorts of exercises - as, guessing one another's thoughts, discovering the defects of some form of expression, repeating long sentences or performing mental calculations. These daily lessons were intended to strengthen memory and reason, and especially to develop the critical sense, and were undoubtedly very beneficial.

My mother descended from one of the oldest families in the country and a line of inventors. Both her father and grandfather originated numerous implements for household, agricultural and other uses. She was a truly great woman,

10

of rare skill, courage and fortitude, who had braved the storms of life and passed thru many a trying experience. When she was sixteen, a virulent pestilence swept the country. Her father was called away to administer the last sacraments to the dying and during his absence she went alone to the assistance of a neighboring family who were stricken by the dread disease. All of the members, five in number succumbed in rapid succession. She bathed, clothed and laid out the bodies, decorating them with flowers according to the custom of the country and when her father returned he found everything ready for a Christian burial.

My mother was an inventor of the first order and would, I believe, have achieved great things had she not been so remote from modern life and its multifold opportunities. She invented and constructed all kinds of tools and devices and wove the finest designs from thread which was spun by her. She even planted seeds, raised the plants and separated the fibres herself. She worked indefatigably, from break of day till late at night, and most of the wearing apparel and furnishings of the home were the product of her hands. When she was past sixty, her fingers were still nimble enough to tie three knots in an eyelash.

There was another and still more important reason for my late awakening. In my boyhood I suffered from a peculiar affliction due to the appearance of images, often accompanied by strong flashes of light, which marred the sight of real objects and interfered with my thoughts and action. They were pictures of things and scenes which I had really seen, never of those imagined. When a word was spoken to me the image of the object it designated would present itself vividly to my vision and sometimes I was quite unable to distinguish whether what I saw was tangible or not. This caused me great discomfort and anxiety. None of the students of psychology or physiology whom I have consulted, could ever explain satisfactorily these phenomena. They seem to have been unique altho I was probably predisposed as I know that my brother experienced a similar trouble. The theory I have formulated is that the images were the result of a reflex action from the brain on the retina under great excitation. They certainly were not hallucinations such as are produced in diseased and anguished minds, for in other respects I was normal and composed. To give an idea of my distress, suppose that I had witnessed a funeral or some such nerve-wracking spectacle. Then, inevitably, in the stillness of night, a vivid picture of the scene would thrust itself before my eyes and persist despite all my efforts to banish it. If my explanation is correct, it should be possible to project on a screen the image of any object one conceives and make it visible. Such an advance would revolutionize all human relations. I am convinced that this wonder can and will be accomplished in time to come. I may add that I have devoted much thought to the solution of the problem.

I have managed to reflect such a picture, which I have seen in my mind, to the mind of another person, in another room. To free myself of these tormenting appearances, I tried to concentrate my mind on something else I had seen, and in this way I would often obtain temporary relief; but in order to get it I had to conjure continuously new images. It was not long before I found that I had exhausted all of those at my command; my 'reel' had run out as it were, because I had seen little of the world--only objects in my home and the immediate surroundings. As I performed these mental operations for the second or third time, in order to chase the appearances from my vision, the remedy gradually lost all its force. Then I instinctively commenced to make excursions beyond the limits of the small world of which I had knowledge, and I saw new scenes. These were at first very blurred and indistinct, and would flit away when I tried to concentrate my attention upon them. They gained in strength

11

and distinctness and finally assumed the concreteness of real things. I soon discovered that my best comfort was attained if I simply went on in my vision further and further, getting new impressions all the time, and so I began to travel; of course, in my mind. Every night, (and sometimes during the day), when alone, I would start on my journeys--see new places, cities and countries; live there, meet people and make friendships and acquaintances and, however unbelievable, it is a fact that they were just as dear to me as those in actual life, and not a bit less intense in their manifestations.

This I did constantly until I was about seventeen, when my thoughts turned seriously to invention. Then I observed to my delight that I could visualize with the greatest facility. I needed no models, drawings or experiments. I could picture them all as real in my mind. Thus I have been led unconsciously to evolve what I consider a new method of materializing inventive concepts and ideas, which is radically opposite to the purely experimental and is in my opinion ever so much more expeditious and efficient.

The moment one constructs a device to carry into practice a crude idea, he finds himself unavoidably engrossed with the details of the apparatus. As he gois on improving and reconstructing, his force of concentration diminishes and he loses sight of the great underlying principle. Results may be obtained, but always at the sacrifice of quality. My method is different. I do not rush into actual work. When I get an idea, I start at once building it up in my imagination. I change the construction, make improvements and operate the device in my mind. It is absolutely immaterial to me whether I run my turbine in thought or test it in my shop. I even note if it is out of balance. There is no difference whatever; the results are the same. In this way I am able to rapidly develop and perfect a conception without touching anything. When I have gone so far as to embody in the invention every possible improvement I can think of and see no fault anywhere, I put into concrete form this final product of my brain. Invariably my device works as I conceived that it should, and the experiment comes out exactly as I planned it. In twenty years there has not been a single exception. Why should it be otherwise? Engineering, electrical and mechanical, is positive in results. There is scarcely a subject that cannot be mathematically treated and the effects calculated or the results determined beforehand, from the available theoretical and practical data. The carrying out into practice of a crude idea as is being generally done, is, I hold, nothing but a waste of energy, money, and time.

My early affliction had however, another compensation. The incessant mental exertion developed my powers of observation and enabled me to discover a truth of great importance. I had noted that the appearance of images was always preceded by actual vision of scenes under peculiar and generally very exceptional conditions, and I was impelled on each occasion to locate the original impulse. After a while this effort grew to be almost automatic and I gained great facility in connecting cause and effect. Soon I became aware, to my surprise, that every thought I conceived was suggested by an external impression. Not only this but all my actions were prompted in a similar way. In the course of time it became perfectly evident to me that I was merely an automation endowed with power OF MOVEMENT RESPONDING TO THE STIMULI OF THE SENSE ORGANS AND THINKING AND ACTING ACCORDINGLY. The practical result of this was the art of telautomatics which has been so far carried out only in an imperfect manner. Its latent possibilities will, however, be eventually shown. I have been years planning self-controlled automata and believe that mechanisms can be produced which will act as if possessed of reason, to a limited degree, and will create a revolution in many commercial and industrial departments. I was about twelve years of age when I first succeeded in banishing an image from my vision by wilful effort, but I never had any control over the flashes of light to which

I have referred. They were, perhaps, my strangest and inexplicable experience. They usually occurred when I found myself in a dangerous or distressing situation or when I was greatly exhilarated. In some instances I have seen all the air around me filled with tongues of living flame. Their intensity, instead of diminishing, increased with time and seemingly attained a maximum when I was about twenty-five years old.

While in Paris in 1883, a prominent French manufacturer sent me an invitation to a shooting expedition which I accepted. I had been long confined to the factory and the fresh air had a wonderfully invigorating effect on me. On my return to the city that night, I felt a positive sensation that my brain had caught fire. I saw a light as tho a small sun was located in it and I passed the whole night applying cold compressions to my tortured head. Finally the flashes diminished in frequency and force but it took more than three weeks before they wholly subsided. When a second invitation was extended to me, my answer was an emphatic NO!

These luminous phenomena still manifest themselves from time to time, as when a new idea opening up possibilities strikes me, but they are no longer exciting, being of relatively small intensity. When I close my eyes I invariably observe first, a background of very dark and uniform blue, not unlike the sky on a clear but starless night. In a few seconds this field becomes animated with innumerable scintillating flakes of green, arranged in several layers and advancing towards me. Then there appears, to the right, a beautiful pattern of two systems of parallel and closely spaced lines, at right angles to one another, in all sorts of colors with yellow, green, and gold predominating. Immediately thereafter, the lines grow brighter and the whole is thickly sprinkled with dots of twinkling light. This picture moves slowly across the field of vision and in about ten seconds vanishes on the left, leaving behind a ground of rather unpleasant and inert grey which quickly gives way to a billowy sea of clouds, seemingly trying to mould themselves into living shapes. It is curious that I cannot project a form into this grey until the second phase is reached. Every time, before falling asleep, images of persons or objects flit before my view. When I see them I know I am about to lose consciousness. If they are absent and refuse to come, it means a sleepless night. To what an extent imagination played a part in my early life, I may illustrate by another odd experience.

Like most children, I was fond of jumping and developed an intense desire to support myself in the air. Occasionally a strong wind richly charged with oxygen blew from the mountains, rendering my body as light as cork and then I would leap and float in space for a long time. It was a delightful sensation and my disappointment was keen when later I undeceived myself. During that period I contracted many strange likes, dislikes and habits, some of which I can trace to external impressions while others are unaccountable. I had a violent aversion against the earrings of women, but other ornaments, as bracelets, pleased me more or less according to design. The sight of a pearl would almost give me a fit, but I was fascinated with the glitter of crystals or objects with sharp edges and plane surfaces. I would not touch the hair of other people except, perhaps at the point of a revolver. I would get a fever by looking at a peach and if a piece of camphor was anywhere in the house it caused me the keenest discomfort. Even now I am not insensible to some of these upsetting impulses. When I drop little squares of paper in a dish filled with liquid, I always sense a peculiar and awful taste in my mouth. I counted the steps in my walks and calculated the cubical contents of soup plates, coffee cups and pieces of food, otherwise my meal was unenjoyable. All repeated acts or operations I performed had to be divisible by three and if I missed I felt impelled to do it all over again, even if it took hours. Up to the age of eight years, my character was weak and vacillating. I had neither courage or strength to form a firm resolve. My feelings came in waves and surges and vibrated unceasingly between extremes. My wishes were of consuming force and like the heads of the hydra, they multiplied. I was oppressed by thoughts of pain in life and death and religious fear. I was swayed by superstitious belief and lived in constant dread of the spirit of evil, of ghosts and ogres and other unholy monsters of the dark. Then all at once, there came a tremendous change which altered the course of my whole existence.

Of all things I liked books best. My father had a large library and whenever I could manage I tried to satisfy my passion for reading. He did not permit it and would fly in a rage when he caught me in the act. He hid the candles when he found that I was reading in secret. He did not want me to spoil my eyes. But I obtained tallow, made the wicking and cast the sticks into tin forms, and every night I would bush the keyhole and the cracks and read, often till dawn, when all others slept and my mother started on her arduous daily task.

On one occasion I came across a novel entitled 'Aoafi,' (the son of Aba), a Serbian translation of a well known Hungarian writer, Josika. This work somehow awakened my dormant powers of will and I began to practice self-control. At first my resolutions faded like snow in April, but in a little while I conquered my weakness and felt a pleasure I never knew before—that of doing as I willed.

In the course of time this vigorous mental exercise became second to nature. At the outset my wishes had to be subdued but gradually desire and will grew to be identical. After years of such discipline I gained so complete a mastery over myself that I toyed with passions which have meant destruction to some of the strongest men. At a certain age I contracted a mania for gambling which greatly worried my parents. To sit down to a game of cards was for me the quintessence of pleasure. My father led an exemplary life and could not excuse the senseless waste of time and money in which I indulged. I had a strong resolve, but my philosophy was bad. I would say to him, 'I can stop whenever I please, but is it worth while to give up that which I would purchase with the joys of Paradise?' On frequent occasions he gave vent to his anger and contempt, but my mother was different. She understood the character of men and knew that one's salvation could only be brought about thru his own efforts. One afternoon, I remember, when I had lost all my money and was craving for a game, she came to me with a roll of bills and said, 'Go and enjoy yourself. The sooner you lose all we possess, the better it will be. I know that you will get over it.' She was right. I conquered my passion then and there and only regretted that it had not been a hundred times as strong. I not only vanquished but tore it from my heart so as not to leave even a trace of desire.

Ever since that time I have been as indifferent to any form of gambling as to picking teeth. During another period I smoked excessively, threatening to ruin my health. Then my will asserted itself and I not only stopped but destroyed all inclination. Long ago I suffered from heart trouble until I discovered that it was due to the innocent cup of coffee I consumed every morning. I discontinued at once, tho I confess it was not an easy task. In this way I checked and bridled other habits and passions, and have not only preserved my life but derived an immense amount of satisfaction from what most men would consider privation and sacrifice.

After finishing the studies at the Polytechnic Institute and University, I had a complete nervous breakdown and while the malady lasted I observed many phenomena, strange and unbelievable...

I shall dwell briefly on these extraordinary experiences, on account of their possible interest to students of psychology and physiology and also because this period of agony was of the greatest consequence on my mental development and subsequent labors. But it is indispensable to first relate the circumstances and conditions which preceded them and in which might be found their partial explanation.

From childhood I was compelled to concentrate attention upon myself. This caused me much suffering, but to my present view, it was a blessing in disguise for it has taught me to appreciate the inestimable value of introspection in the preservation of life, as well as a means of achievement. The pressure of occupation and the incessant stream of impressions pouring into our consciousness thru all the gateways of knowledge make modern existence hazardous in many ways. Most persons are so absorbed in the contemplation of the outside world that they are wholly oblivious to what is passing on within themselves. The premature death of millions is primarily traceable to this cause. Even among those who exercise care, it is a common mistake to avoid imaginary, and ignore the real dangers. And what is true of an individual also applies, more or less, to a people as a whole.

Abstinence was not always to my liking, but I find ample reward in the agreeable experiences I am now making. Just in the hope of converting some to my precepts and convictions I will recall one or two.

A short time ago I was returning to my hotel. It was a bitter cold night, the ground slippery, and no taxi to be had. Half a block behind me followed another man, evidently as anxious as myself to get under cover. Suddenly my legs went up in the air. At the same instant there was a flash in my brain. The nerves responded, the muscles contracted. I swung thru 180 degrees and landed on my hands. I resumed my walk as tho nothing had happened when the stranger caught up with me. "How old are you?" he asked, surveying me critically.

"Oh, about fifty-nine," I replied. "What of it?"

"Well," said he, "I have seen a cat do this but never a man." About a month ago I wanted to order new eye glasses and went to an oculist who put me thru the usual tests. He looked at me incredulously as I read off with ease the smallest print at considerable distance. But when I told him I was past sixty he gasped in astonishment. Friends of mine often remark that my suits fit me like gloves but they do not know that all my clothing is made to measurements which were taken nearly fifteen years ago and never changed. During this same period my weight has not varied one pound. In this connection I may tell a funny story.

One evening, in the winter of 1885, Mr. Edison, Edward H. Johnson, the President of the Edison Illuminating Company, Mr. Batchellor, Manager of the works, and myself, entered a little place opposite 65 Firth Avenue, where the offices of the company were located. Someone suggested guessing weights and I was induced to step on a scale. Edison felt me all over and said: "Tesla weighs 152 lbs. to an ounce," and he guessed it exactly. Stripped I weighed 142 pounds, and that is still my weight. I whispered to Mr. Johnson; "How is it possible that Edison could guess my weight so closely?"

15

"Well," he said, lowering his voice. "I will tell you confidentially, but you must not say anything. He was employed for a long time in a Chicago slaughter-house where he weighed thousands of hogs every day. That's why."

Mr friend, the Hon. Chauncey M. Dupew, tells of an Englishman on whom he sprung one of his original anecdotes and who listened with a puzzled experssion, but a year later, laughed out loud. I will frankly confess it took me longer than that to appreciate Johnson's joke. Now, my well-being is simply the result of a careful and measured mode of living and perhaps themost astonishing thing is that three times in my youth I was rendered by illness a hopeless physical wreck and given up by physicians. MORE than this, thru ignorance and lightheartedness, I got into all sorts of difficulties, dangers and scrapes from which I extricated myself as by enchantment. I was almost drowned a dozen times; was nearly boiled alive and just missed being cremated. I was entombed, lost and frozen. I had hair-breadth escapes from mad dogs, hogs, and other wild animals. I passed thru dreadful diseases and met with all kinds of odd mishaps and that I am hale and hearty today seems like a miracle. But as I recall these incidents to my mind I feel convinced that my preservation was not altogether accidental, but was indeed the work of divine power. An inventor's endeavor is essentially life saving. Whether he harnesses forces, improves devices, or provides new comforts and conveniences, he is adding to the safety of our existence. He is also better qualified than the average individual to protect himself in peril, for he is observant and resourceful. If I had no other evidence that I was, in a measure, possessed of such qualities, I would find it in these personal experiences. The reader will be able to judge for himself if I mention one or two instances.

On one occasion, when about fourteen years old, I wanted to scare some friends who were bathing with me. My plan was to dive under a long floating structure and slip out quietly at the other end. Swimming and diving came to me as naturally as to a duck and I was confident that I could perform the feat. Accordingly I plunged into the water and, when out of view, turned around and proceeded rapidly towards the opposite side. Thinking that I was safely beyond the structure, I rose to the surface but to my dismay struck a beam. Of course, I quickly dived and forged ahead with rapid strokes until my breath was beginning to give out. Rising for the second time, my head came again in contact with a beam. Now I was becoming desperate. However, summoning all my energy, I made a third frantic attempt but the result was the same. The torture of suppressed breathing was getting unendurable, my brain was reeling and I felt myself sinking. At that moment, when my situation seemed absolutely hopeless, I experienced one of those flashes of light and the structure above me appeared before my vision. I either discerned or guessed that there was a little space between the surface of the water and the boards resting on the beams and, with consciousness nearly gone, I floated up, pressed my mouth close to the planks and managed to inhale a little air, unfortunately mingled with a spray of water which nearly choked me. Several times I repeated this procedure as in a dream until my heart, which was racing at a terrible rate, quieted down, and I gained composure. After that I made a number of unsuccessful dives, having completely lost the sense of direction, but finally succeeded in getting out of the trap when my friends had already given me up and were fishing for my body. That bathing season was spoiled for me thru recklessness but I soon forgot the lesson and only two years later I fell into a worse predicament.

There was a large flour mill with a dam across the river near the city where I was studying at that time. As a rule the height of the water was only two or three inches above the dam and to swim to it was a sport not very dangerous in which I often indulged. One day I went alone to the river to enjoy

16

myself as usual. When I was a short distance from the masonry, however, I was horrified to observe that the water had risen and was carrying me along swiftly. I tried to get away but it was too late. Luckily, tho, I saved myself from being swept over by taking hold of the wall with both hands. The pressure against my chest was great and I was barely able to keep my head above the surface. Not a soul was in sight and my voice was lost in the roar of the fall. Slowly and gradually I became exhausted and unable to withstand the strain longer. Just as I was about to let go, to be dashed against the rocks below, I saw in a flash of light a familiar diagram illustrating the hydraulic principle that the pressure of a fluid in motion is proportionate to the area exposed and automatically I turned on my left side. As if by magic, the pressure was reduced and I found it comparatively easy in that position to resist the force of the stream. But the danger still confronted me. I knew that sooner or later I would be carried down, as it was not possible for any help to reach me in time, even if I had attracted attention. I am ambidextrous now, but then I was left-handed and had comparatively little strength in my right arm. For this reason I did not dare to turn on the other side to rest and nothing remained but to slowly push my body along the dam. I had to get away from the mill towards which my face was turned, as the current there was much swifter and deeper. It was a long and painful ordeal and I came near to failing at its very end, for I was confronted with a depression in the masonry. I managed to get over with the last ounce of my strength and fell in a swoon when I reached the bank, where I was found. I had torn virtually all the skin from my left side and it took several weeks before the fever had subsided and I was well. These are only two of many instances, but they may be sufficient to show that had it not been for the inventor's instinct, I would not have lived to tell the tale.

Interested people have often asked me how and when I began to invent. This I can only answer from my present recollection in the light of which, the first attempt I recall was rather ambitious for it involved the invention of an apparatus and a method. In the former I was anticipated, but the latter was original. It happened in this way. One of my playmates had come into the possession of a hook and fishing tackle which created quite an excitement in the village, and the next morning all started out to catch frogs. I was left alone and deserted owing to a quarrel with this boy. I had never seen a real hook and pictured it as something wonderful, endowed with peculiar qualities, and was despairing not to be one of the party. Urged by necessity, I somehow got hold of a piece of soft iron wire, hammered the end to a sharp point between two stones, bent it into shape, and fastened it to a strong string. I then cut a rod, gathered some bait, and went down to the brook where there were frogs in abundance. But I could not catch any and was almost discouraged when it occurred to me to dangle the empty hook in front of a frog sitting on a stump. At first he collapsed but by and by his eyes bulged out and became bloodshot, he swelled to twice his normal size and made a vicious snap at the hook. Immediately I pulled him up. I tried the same thing again and again and the method proved infallible. When my comrades, who in spite of their fine outfit had caught nothing, came to me, they were green with envy. For a long time I kept my secret and enjoyed the monopoly but finally yielded to the spirit of Christmas. Every boy could then do the same and the following summer brought disaster to the frogs.

In my next attempt, I seem to have acted under the first instinctive impulse which later dominated me,-- to harness the energies of nature to the service of man. I did this thru the medium of May bugs, or June bugs as they are called in America, which were a veritable pest in that country and sometimes broke the branches of trees by the sheer weight of their bodies. The bushes were black with them. I would attach as many as four of them to a cross-piece, rotably arranged on a thin spindle, and transmit the motion of the same to a large disc and so derive considerable 'power.' These creatures were remarkably efficient, for once they were started, they had no sense to stop and continued whirling for hours and hours and the hotter it was, the harder they worked. All went well until a strange boy came to the place. He was the son of a retired officer in the Austrian army. That urchin ate May-bugs alive and enjoyed them as tho they were the finest blue-point oysters. That disgusting sight terminated my endeavors in this promising field and I have never since been able to touch a May-bug or any other insect for that matter.

After that, I believe, I undertook to take apart and assemble the clocks of my grand-father. In the former operation I was always successful, but often failed in the latter. So it came that he brought my work to a sudden halt in a manner not too delicate and it took thirty years before I tackled another clockwork again.

Shortly thereafter, I went into the manufacture of a kind of pop-gun which comprised a hollow tube, a piston, and two plugs of hemp. When firing the gun, the piston was pressed against the stomach and the tube was pushed back quickly with both hands. The air between the plugs was compressed and raised to high temperature and one of them was expelled with a loud report. The art consisted in selecting a tube of the proper taper from the hollow stalks which were found in our garden. I did very well with that gun, but my activities interfered with the window panes in our house and met with painful discouragement.

If I remember rightly, I then took to carving swords from pieces of furniture which I could conveniently obtain. At that time I was under the sway of the Serbian national poetry and full of admiration for the feats of the heroes. I used to spend hours in mowing down my enemies in the form of corn-stalks which ruined the crops and netted me several spankings from my mother. More-over, these were not of the formal kind but the genuine article.

I had all this and more behind me before I was six years old and had passed thru one year of elementary school in the village of Smiljan where my family lived. At this juncture we moved to the little city of Gospic nearby. This change of residence was like a calamity to me. It almost broke my heart to part from our pigeons, chickens and sheep, and our magnificent flock of geese which used to rise to the clouds in the morning and return from the feed-ing grounds at sundown in battle formation, so perfect that it would have put a squadron of the best aviators of the present day to shame. In our new house I was but a prisoner, watching the strange people I saw thru the window blinds. My bashfulness was such that I would rather have faced a roaring lion than one of the city dudes who strolled about. But my hardest trial came on Sunday when I had to dress up and attend the service. There I met with an accident, the mere thought of which made my blood curdle like sour milk for years after-wards. It was my second adventure in a church. Not long before, I was en-tombed for a night in an old chapel on an inaccessible mountain which was visited only once a year. It was an awful experience, but this one was worse.

There was a wealthy lady in town, a good but pompous woman, who used to come to the church gorgeously painted up and attired with an enormous train and attendants. One Sunday I had just finished ringing the bell in the belfry and rushed downstairs, when this grand dame was sweeping out and I jumped on her train. It tore off with a ripping noise which sounded like a salvo of musketry

18

fired by raw recruits. My father was livid with rage. He gave me a gentle slap on the cheek, the only corporal punishment he ever administered to me, but I almost feel it now. The embarrassment and confusion that followed are indescribable. I was practically ostracised until something else happened which redeemed me in the estimation of the community.

An enterprising young merchant had organized a fire department. A new fire engine was purchased, uniforms provided and the men drilled for service and parade. The engine was beautifully painted red and black. One afternoon, the official trial was prepared for and the machine was transported to the river. The entire population turned out to witness the great spectacle. When all the speeches and ceremonies were concluded, the command was given to pump, but not a drop of water came from the nozzle. The professors and experts tried in vain to locate the trouble. The fizzle was complete when I arrived at the scene. My knowledge of the mechanism was nil and I knew next to nothing of air pressure, but instinctively I felt for the suction hose in the water and found that it had collapsed. When I waded in the river and opened it up, the water rushed forth and not a few Sunday clothes were spoiled. Archimedes running naked thru the streets of Syracuse and shouting Eureka at the top of his voice did not make a greater impression than myself. I was carried on the shoulders and was the hero of the day.

Upon settling in the city I began a four years course in the so-called Normal School preparatory to my studies at the College or Real-Gymnasium. During this period my boyish efforts and exploits as well as troubles, continued.

Among other things, I attained the unique distinction of champion crow catcher in the country. My method of procedure was extremely simple. I would go into the forest, hide in the bushes, and imitate the call of the birds. Usually I would get several answers and in a short while a crow would flutter down into the shrubbery near me. After that, all I needed to do was to throw a piece of cardboard to detract its attention, jump up and grab it before it could extricate itself from the undergrowth. In this way I would capture as many as I desired. But on one occasion something occurred which made me respect them. I had caught a fine pair of birds and was returning home with a friend. When we left the forest, thousands of crows had gathered making a frightful racket. In a few minutes they rose in pursuit and soon enveloped us. The fun lasted until all of a sudden I received a blow on the back of my head which knocked me down. Then they attacked me viciously. I was compelled to release the two birds and was glad to join my friend who had taken refuge in a cave.

In the school room there were a few mechanical models which interested me and turned my attention to water turbines. I constructed many of these and found great pleasure in operating them. How extraordinary was my life an incident may illustrate. My uncle had no use for this kind of pastime and more than once rebuked me. I was fascinated by a description of Niagara Falls I had perused, and pictured in my imagination a big wheel run by the Falls. I told my uncle that I would go to America and carry out this scheme. Thirty years later I saw my ideas carried out at Niagara and marveled at the unfathomable mystery of the mind.

I made all kinds of other contrivances and contraptions but among those, the arbalests I produced were the best. My arrows, when shot, disappeared from sight and at close range traversed a plank of pine one inch thick. Thru the continuous tightening of the bows I developed skin on my stomach much like that of a crocodile and I am often wondering whether it is due to this exercise that I am able even now to digest cobble-stones! Nor can I pass in silence my performances with the sling which would have enabled me to give a stunning exhibit at the Hippodrome. And now I will tell of one of my feats with this unique implement of war which will strain to the utmost the credulity of the reader.

I was practicing while walking with my uncle along the river. The sun was setting, the trout were playful and from time to time one would shoot up into the air, its glistening body sharply defined against a projecting rock beyond. Of course any boy might have hit a fish under these propitious conditions but I undertook a much more difficult task and I foretold to my uncle, to the minutest detail, what I intended doing. I was to hurl a stone to meet the fish, press its body against the rock, and cut it in two. It was no sooner said than done. My uncle looked at me almost scared out of his wits and exclaimed "Vade retra Satanae!" and it was a few days before he spoke to me again. Other records, however great, will be eclipsed but I feel that I could peacefully rest on my laurels for a thousand years.

# HOW TESLA CONCEIVED "THE ROTARY MAGNETIC FIELD"

At the age of ten I entered the Real gymnasium which was a new and fairly well equipped institution. In the department of physics were various models of classical scientific apparatus, electrical and mechanical. The demonstrations and experiments performed from time to time by the instructors fascinated me and were undoubtedly a powerful incentive to invention. I was also passionately fond of mathematical studies and often won the professor's praise for rapid calculation. This was due to my acquired facility of visualizing the figures and performing the operation, not in the usual intuitive manner, but as in actual life. Up to a certain degree of complexity it was absolutely the same to me whether I wrote the symbols on the board or conjured them before my mental vision. But freehand drawing, to which many hours of the course were devoted, was an annoyance I could not endure. This was rather remarkable as most of the members of the family excelled in it. Perhaps my aversion was simply due to the predilection I found in undisturbed thought. Had it not been for a few exceptionally stupid boys, who could not do anything at all, my record would have been the worst.

It was a serious handicap as under the then existing educational regime drawing being obligatory, this deficiency threatened to spoil my whole career and my father had considerable trouble in rail-roading me from one class to another.

In the second year at that institution I became obsessed with the idea of producing continuous motion thru steady air pressure. The pump incident, of which I have told, had set afire my youthful imagination and impressed me with the boundless possibilities of a vacuum. I grew frantic in my desire to harness this inexhaustible energy but for a long time I was groping in the dark. Finally, however, my endeavors crystallized in an invention which was to enable me to achieve what no other mortal ever attempted. Imagine a cylinder freely rotatable on two bearings and partly surrounded by a rectangular trough which fits it perfectly. The open side of the trough is enclosed by a partition so that the cylindrical segment within the enclosure divides the latter into two compartments entirely separated from each other by air-tight sliding joints. One of these compartments being sealed and once for all exhausted, the other remaining open, a perpetual rotation of the cylinger would result. At least, so I thought.

A wooden model was constructed and fitted with infinite care and when I applied the pump on one side and actually observed that there was a tendency to turning, I was delirious with joy. Mechanical flight was the one thing I wanted to accomplish altho still under the discouraging recollection of a bad fall I sustained by jumping with an umbrella from the top of a building. Every day I used to transport myself thru the air to distant regions but could not understand just how I managed to do it. Now I had something concrete, a flying machine with nothing more than a rotating shaft, flapping wings, and;- a vacuum of unlimited power! From that time on I made my daily aerial excursions in a vehicle of comfort and luxury as might have befitted King Solomon. It took years before I understood that the atmospheric pressure acted at right angles to the surface of the cylinder and that the slight rotary effort I observed was due to a leak! Tho this knowledge came gradually it gave me a painful shock.

I had hardly completed my course at the Real Gymnasium when I was pros-
trated with a dangerous illness or rather, a score of them, and my condition
became so desperate that I was given up by physicians. During this period I
was permitted to read constantly, obtaining books from the Public Library which
had been neglected and entrusted to me for classification of the works and
preparation of catalogues.

One day I was handed a few volumes of new literature unlike anything I
had ever read before and so captivating as to make me utterly forget my hopeless state. They were the earlier works of Mark Twain and to them might have
been due the miraculous recovery which followed. Twenty-five years later, when
I met Mr. Clements and we formed a friendship between us, I told him of the
experience and was amazed to see that great man of laughter burst into tears..
My studies were continued at the higher Real Gymnasium in Carlstadt,
Croatia, where one of my aunts resided. She was a distinguished lady, the
wife of a Colonel who was an old war-horse having participated in many battles.
I can never forget the three years I passed at their home. No fortress in
time of war was under a more rigid discipline. I was fed like a canary bird.
All the meals were of the highest quality and deliciously prepared, but short
in quantity by a thousand per cent. The slices of ham cut by my aunt were
like tissue paper. When the Colonel would put something substantial on my
plate she would snatch it away and say excitedly to him; "Be careful. Niko is
very delicate."

I had a voracious appetite and suffered like Tantalus.

But I lived in an atmosphere of refinement and artistic taste quite unusual for those times and conditions. The land was low and marshy and malaria
fever never left me while there despite the enormous amounts of quinine I consumed. Occasionally the river would rise and drive an army of rats into the
buildings, devouring everything, even to the bundles of fierce paprika. These
pests were to me a welcome diversion. I thinned their ranks by all sorts of
means, which won me the unenviable distinction of rat-catcher in the community.
At last, however, my course was completed, the misery ended, and I obtained the
certificate of maturity which brought me to the cross-roads.

During all those years my parents never wavered in their resolve to make
me embrace the clergy, the mere thought of which filled me with dread. I had
become intensely interested in electricity under the stimulating influence of
my Professor of Physics, who was an ingenious man and often demonstrated the
principles by apparatus of his own invention. Among these I recall a device
in the shape of a freely rotatable bulb, with tinfoil coatings, which was made
to spin rapidly when connected to a static machine. It is impossible for me
to convey an adequate idea of the intensity of feeling I experienced in witnes-
sing his exhibitions of these mysterious phenomena, Every impression produced
a thousand echoes in my mind. I wanted to know more of this wonderful force;
I longed for experiment and investigation and resigned myself to the inevitable with aching heart. Just as I was making ready for the long journey home
I received word that my father wished me to go on a shooting expedition. It
was a strange request as he had been always strenuously opposed to this kind
of sport. But a few days later I learned that the cholera was raging in that
district and, taking advantage of an opportunity, I returned to Gospic in dis-
regard to my parent's wishes. It is incredible how absolutely ignorant people
were as to the causes of this scourge which visited the country in intervals of
from fifteen to twenty years. They thought that the deadly agents were transmitted thru the air and filled it with pungent odors and smoke. In the meantime they drank the infested water and died in heaps. I contracted the dreadful

disease on the very day of my arrival and altho surviving the crisis, I was confined to bed for nine months with scarcely any ability to move. My energy was completely exhausted and for the second time I found myself at Death's door.

In one of the sinking spells which was thought to be the last, my father rushed into the room. I still see his pallid face as he tried to cheer me in tones belying his assurance. "Perhaps," I said, "I may get well if you will let me study engineering." "You will go to the best technical institution in the world," he solemnly replied, and I knew that he meant it. A heavy weight was lifted from my mind but the relief would have come too late had it not been for a mravelous cure brought about thru a bitter decoction of a peculiar bean. I came to life like another Lazarus to the utter amazement of everybody.

My father insisted that I spend a year in healthful physical outdoor exercise to which I reluctantly consented. For most of this term I roamed in the mountains, loaded with a hunter's outfit and a bundle of books, and this contact with nature made me stronger in body as well as in mind. I thought and planned, and conceived many ideas almost as a rule delusive. The vision was clear enough but the knowledge of principles was very limited.

In one of my inventions I proposed to convey letters and packages across the seas, thru a submarine tube, in spherical containers of sufficient strength to resist the hydraulic pressure. The pumping plant, intended to force the water thru the tube, was accurately figured and designed and all other particulars carefully worked out. Only one trifling detail, of no consequence, was lightly dismissed. I assumed an arbitrary velocity of the water and, what is more, took pleasure in making it high, thus arriving at a stupendous performance supported by faultless calculations. Subsequent reflections, however, on the resistance of pipes to fluid flow induced me to make this invention public property.

Another one of my projects was to construct a ring around the equator which would, of course, float freely and could be arrested in its spinning motion by reactionary forces, thus enabling travel at a rate of about one thousand miles an hour, impracticable by rail. The reader will smile. The plan was difficult of execution, I will admit, but not nearly so bad as that of a well known New York professor, who wanted to pump the air from the torrid to the temperate zones, entirely forgetful of the fact that the Lord had provided a gigantic machine for this purpose.

Still another scheme, far more important and attractive, was to derive power from the rotational energy of terrestrial bodies. I had discovered that objects on the earth's surface owing to the diurnal rotation of the globe, are carried by the same alternately in and against the direction of translatory movement. From this results a great change in momentum which could be utilized in the simplest imaginable manner to furnish motive effort in any habitable region of the world. I cannot find words to describe my disappointment when later I realized that I was in the predicament of Archimedes, who vainly sought for a fixed point in the Universe.

At the termination of my vacation I was sent to the POLY-TECHNIC School in Gratz, Styria (Austria), which my father had chosen as one of the oldest and best reputed institutions. That was the moment I had eagerly awaited and I began my studies under good auspices and firmly resolved to succeed. My previous training was above the average, due to my father's teaching and opportunities afforded. I had acquired the knowledge of a number of languages and waded thru the books of several libraries, picking up information more or less useful.  Then again, for the first time, I could choose my subjects as I liked, and free-hand drawing was to bother me no more.

I had made up my mind to give my parents a surprise, and during the whole first year I regularly started my work at three o'clock in the morning and continued until eleven at night, no Sundays or holidays excepted.  As most of my fellow-students took things easily, naturally I eclipsed all records.  In the course of the year I passed thru nine exams and the professors thought I deserved more than the highest qualifications.  Armed with their flattering certificates, I went home for a short rest, expecting a triumph, and was mortified when my father made light of these hard-won honors.

That almost killed my ambition; but later, after he had died, I was pained to find a package of letters which the professors had written to him to the effect that unless he took me away from the Institution I would be killed thru overwork.  Thereafter I devoted myself chiefly to physics, mechanics and mathematical studies, spending the hours of leisure in the libraries.

I had a veritable mania for finishing whatever I began, which often got me into difficulties.  On one occasion I started to read the works of Voltaire, when I learned, to my dismay that there were close to one hundred large volumes in small print which that monster had written while drinking seventytwo cups of black coffee per diem.  It had to be done, but when I laid aside the last book I was very glad, and said, "Never more!"

My first year's showing had won me the appreciation and friendship of several professors.  Among these, Professor Rogner, who was teaching arithmetical subjects and geometry; Professor Poeschl, who held the chair of theoretical and experimental physics, and Dr. Alle, who taught integral calculus and specialized in differential equations.  This scientist was the most brilliant lecturer to whom I ever listened.  He took a special interest in my progress and would frequently remain for an hour or two in the lecture room, giving me problems to solve, in which I delighted.  To him I explained a flying machine I had conceived, not an illusionary invention, but one based on sound, scientific principles, which has become realizable thru my turbine and will soon be given to the world.  Both Professors Rogner and Poeschl were curious men.  The former had peculiar ways of expressing himself and whenever he did so, there was a riot, followed by a long and embarrassing pause.  Prof. Poeschl was a methodical and thoroughly grounded German.  He had enormous feet, and hands like the paws of a bear, but all of his experiments were skillfully performed with clocklike precision and without a miss.  It was in the second year of my studies that we received a Gramme Dynamo from Paris, having the horseshoe form of a laminated field magnet, and a wire wound armature with a commutator.  It was connected up and various effects of the currents were shown.  While Prof. Poeschl was making demonstrations, running the machine was a motor, the brushes gave trouble, sparking badly, and I observed that it might be possible to operate a motor without these appliances.  But he declared that it could not be done and did me the honour of delivering a lecture on the subject, at the conclusion of which he remarked, 'Mr. Tesla may accomplish great things, but he certainly will never do this.  It would be equivalent to converting a steadily pulling force, like that of gravity into a rotary effort.  It is a perpetual motion scheme, an impossible idea.'  But instinct is something which transcends knowledge.  We have, undoubtedly, certain finer fibers that enable us to perceive truths when logical deduction, or any other willful effort of the brain, is futile.

For a time I wavered, impressed by the professor's authority, but soon became convinced I was right and undertook the task with all the fire and bound-less confidence of youth. I started by first picturing in my mind a direct-current machine, running it and following the changing flow of the currents in the armature. Then I would imagine an alternator and investigate the prog-resses taking place in a similar manner. Next I would visualize systems comprising motors and generators and operate them in various ways.

The images I saw were to me perfectly real and tangible. All my remain-ing term in Gratz was passed in intense but fruitless efforts of this kind, and I almost came to the conclusion that the problem was insolvable.

In 1880 I went to Prague, Bohemia, carrying out my father's wish to complete my education at the University there. It was in that city that I made a decided advance, which consisted in detaching the commutator from the machine and studying the phenomena in this new aspect, but still without result. In the year following there was a sudden change in my views of life.

I realized that my parents had been making too great sacrifices on my account and resolved to relieve them of the burden. The wave of the American telephone had just reached the European continent and the system was to be installed in Budapest, Hungary. It appeared an ideal opportunity, all the more as a friend of our family was at the head of the enterprise.

It was here that I suffered the complete breakdown of the nerves to which I have referred. What I experienced during the period of that illness surpasses all belief. My sight and hearing were always extraordinary. I could clearly discern objects in the distance when others saw no trace of them. Several times in my boyhood I saved the houses of our neighbours from fire by hearing the faint crackling sounds which did not distrub their sleep, and calling for help. In 1899, when I was past forty and carrying on my experiments in Colorado, I could hear very distinctly thunderclaps at a dis-tance of 550 miles. The limit of audition for my young assistants was scarce-ly more than 150 miles. My ear was thus over thirteen times more sensitive, yet at that time I was, so to speak, stone deaf in comparison with the acute-ness of my hearing while under the nervous strain.

In Budapest I could hear the ticking of a watch with three rooms between me and the time-piece. A fly alighting on a table in the room would cause a dull thud in my ear. A carriage passing at a distance of a few miles fairly shook my whole body. The whistle of a locomotive twenty or thirty miles away made the bench or chair on which I sat, vibrate so strongly that the pain was unbearable. The ground under my feet trembled continuously. I had to support my bed on rubber cushions to get any rest at all. The roaring noises from near and far often produced the effect of spoken words which would have fright-ened me had I not been able to resolve them into their accumulated components. The sun rays, when periodically intercepted, would cause blows of such force on my brain that they would stun me. I had to summon all my will power to pass under a bridge or other structure, as I experienced a crushing pressure on the skull. In the dark I had the sense of a bat, and could detect the presence of an object at a distance of twelve feet by a peculiar creepy sen-sation on the forehead. My pulse varied from a few to two hundred and sixty beats and all the tissues of the body with twitchings and tremors, which was perhaps the hardest to bear. A renowned physician who gave me daily large doses of Bromide of Potassium, pronounced my malady unique and incurable.

It is my eternal regret that I was not under the observation of experts in physiology and psychology at that time. I clung desperately to life, but never expected to recover. Can anyone believe that so hopeless a physical wreck could ever be transformed into a man of astonishing strength and tenacity; able to work thirty-eight years almost without a day's interruption, and find himself still strong and fresh in body and mind? Such is my case. A powerful desire to live and to continue the work, and the assistance of a devoted friend, an athlete, accomplished the wonder. My health returned and with it the vigor of mind.

In attacking the problem again, I almost regretted that the struggle was soon to end. I had so much energy to spare. When I understood the task, it was not with a resolve such as men often make. With me it was a sacred vow, a question of life and death. I knew that I would perish if I failed. Now I felt that the battle was won. Back in the deep recesses of the brain was the solution, but I could not yet give it outward expression.

One afternoon, which is ever present in my recollection, I was enjoying a walk with my friend in the City Park and reciting poetry. At that age, I knew entire books by heart, word for word. One of these was Goethe's 'Faust.' The sun was just setting and reminded me of the glorious passage, 'Sie ruckt und weicht, der Tag ist uberlebt, Dort eilt sie hin und fordert neues Leben. Oh, dase kein Flugel mich vom Boden hebt Ihr nach und immer nach zu streben! Ein schoner Traum indessen sie entweicht, Ach, au des Geistes Flugein wird so leicht Kein korperlicher Flugel sich gesellen!' As I uttered these inspiring words the idea came like a flash of lightning and in an instant the truth was revealed. I drew with a stick on the sand, the diagram shown six years later in my address before the American Institute of Electrical Engineers, and my companion understood them perfectly. The images I saw were wonderfully sharp and clear and had the solidity of metal and stone, so much so that I told him, 'See my motor here; watch me reverse it.' I cannot begin to describe my emotions. Pygmalion seeing his statue come to life could not have been more deeply moved. A thousand secrets of nature which I might have stumbled upon accidentally, I would have given for that one which I had wrested from her against all odds and at the peril of my existance......

# THE DISCOVERY OF THE TESLA COIL AND TRANSFORMER

## (THE BASIC PART OF EVERY RADIO AND T.V.)

For a while I gave myself up entirely to the intense enjoyment of picturing machines and devising new forms.  It was a mental state of happiness about
as complete as I have ever known in life.  Ideas came in an uninterrupted
stream and the only difficulty I had was to hold them fast.  The pieces of
apparatus I conceived were to me absolutely real and tangible in every detail,
even to the minutest marks and signs of wear.  I delighted in imagining the
motors constantly running, for in this way they presented to the mind's eye
a more fascinating sight.  When natural inclination develops into a passionate
desire, one advances towards his goal in seven-league boots.  In less than two
months I evolved virtually all the types of motors and modifications of the
system which are now identified with my name, and which are used under many
other names all over the world.  It was, perhaps, providential that the necessities of existence commanded a temporary halt to this consuming acitivty
of the mind.

I came to Budapest prompted by a premature report concerning the telephone enterprise and, as irony of fate willed it, I had to accept a position
as draftsman in the Central Telegraph Office of the Hungarian Government at
a salary which I deem it my privilege not to disclose.  Fortunately, I soon
won the interest of the Inspector-in-Chief and was thereafter employed on
calculations, designs and estimates in connection with new installations,
until the Telephone Exchange was started, when I took charge of the same.
The knowledge and practical experience I gained in the course of this work,
was most valuable and the employment gave me ample opportunities for the
exercise of my inventive faculties.  I made several improvements in the
Central Station apparatus and perfected a telephone repeater or amplifier
which was never patented or publicly described but would be creditable to me
even today.  In recognition of my efficient assistance the organizer of the
undertaking, Mr. Puskas, upon disposing of his business in Budapest, offered
me a position in Paris which I gladly accepted.

I never can forget the deep impression that magic city produced on my
mind.  For several days after my arrival, I roamed thru the streets in utter
bewilderment of the new spectacle.  The attractions were many and irresistible, but, alas, the income was spent as soon as received.  When Mr. Puskas
asked me how I was getting along in the new sphere, I described the situation
accurately in the statement that 'The last twenty-nine days of the month are
the toughest.'  I led a rather strenucus life in what would now be termed--
'Rooseveltian fashion.'  Every morning, regardless of the weather, I would go
from the Boulevard St. Marcel, where I resided, to a bathing house on the
Seine; plunge into the water, loop the circuit twenty-seven times and then
walk an hour to reach Ivry, where the Company's factory was located.  There I
would have a wood-chopper's breakfast at half-past seven o'clock and then
eagerly await the lunch hour, in the meanwhile cracking hard nuts for the
Manager of the Works, Mr. Charles Batchellor, who was an intimate friend and
assistant of Edison.  Here I was thrown in contact with a few Americans who
fairly fell in love with me because of my proficiency in Billiards!  To these
men I explained my invention and one of them, Mr. D. Cunningham, foreman of

the Mechanical Department, offered to form a stock company. The proposal seemed to me comical in the extreme. I did not have the faintest conception of what that meant, except that it was an American way of doing things. Nothing came of it, however, and during the next few months I had to travel from one place to another in France and Germany to cure the ills of the power plants.

On my return to Paris, I submitted to one of the administrators of the Company, Mr. Rau, a plan for improving their dynamos and was given an opportunity. My success was complete and the delighted directors accorded me the privilege of developing automatic regulators which were much desired. Shortly after, there was some trouble with the lighting plant which had been installed at the new railroad station in Strassburg, Alsace. The wiring was defective and on the occasion of the opening ceremonies, a large part of a wall was blown out thru a short-circuit, right in the presence of old Emperor William 1. The German Government refused to take the plant and the French Company was facing a serious loss. On account of my knowledge of the German language and past experience, I was entrusted with the difficult task of straightening out matters and early in 1883, I went to Strasburg on that mission.

Some of the incidents in that city have left an indelible record on my memory. By a curious coincidence, a number of the men who subsequently achieved fame, lived there about that time. In later life I used to say,'There were bacteria of greatness in that old town.' Others caught the disease, but I escaped!' The practical work, correspondence, and conferences with officials kept me preoccupied day and night, but as soon as I was able to manage, I undertook the construction of a simple motor in a mechanical shop opposit the railroad station, having brought with me from Paris some material for that purpose. The consumation of the experiment was, however, delayed until the summer of that year, when I finally had the satisfaction of seeing the rotation effected by alternating currents of different phase, and without sliding contacts or commutator, as I had conceived a year before. It was an exquisite pleasure but not to compare with the delirium of joy following the first revelation.

Among my new friends was the former Mayor of the city, Mr. Sauzin, whom I had already, in a measure, acquainted with this and other inventions of mine and whose support I endeavored to enlist. He was sincerely devoted to me and put my project before several wealthy persons, but to my mortificaiton, found no response. He wanted to help me in every possible way and the approach of the first of July, 1917, happens to remind me of a form of 'assistance' I received from that charming man, which was not financial, but none the less appreciated. In 1870, when the Germans invaded the country, Mr. Sauzin had buried a good sized allotment of St. Estephe of 1801 and he came to the conclusion that he knew no worthier person than myself, to consume that precious beverage. This, I may say, is one of the unforgetable incidents to which I have referred. My friend urged me to return to Paris as soon as possible and seek support there. This I was anxious to do, but my work and negotiations were protracted, owing to all sorts of petty obstacles I encountered, so that at times the situation seemed hopeless. Just to give an idea of German thoroughness and 'efficiency,' I may mention here a rather funny experience.

An incandescent lamp of 16 c.p. was to be placed in a hallway, and upon selecting the proper location, I ordered the 'monteur' to run the wires. After working for a while, he concluded that the engineer had to be consulted and this was done. The latter made several objections but ultimately agreed that the lamp should be placed two inches from the spot I had assigned, whereupon the work proceeded. Then the engineer became worried and told me that Inspector Averdeck should be notified. That important person was called, he investigated, debated, and decided that the lamp should be shifted back two inches, which was the place I had marked! It was not long, however, before Averdeck got cold feet himself and advised me that he had informed Ober-Inspector Hieronimus of the matter and that I should await his decision. It was several days before the Ober-Inspector was able to free himself of other pressing duties, but at last he arrived and a two hour debate followed, when he decided to move the lamp two inches further. My hopes that this was the final act, were shattered when the Ober-Inspector returned and said to me, 'Regierungsrath Funke is so particular that I would not dare to give an order for placing this lamp without his explicit approval.' Accordingly, arrangements for a visit from that great man were made. We started cleaning up and polishing early in the morning, and when Funke came with his retinue he was ceremoniously received. After two hours deliberation, he suddenly exclaimed, 'I must be going!,' and pointing to a place on the ceiling, he ordered me to put the lamp there. It was the exact spot which I had originally chosen! So it went day after day with variations, but I was determined to achieve, at whatever cost, and in the end my efforts were rewarded.

By the spring of 1884, all the differences were adjusted, the plant formally accepted, and I returned to Paris with pleasing anticipation. One of the administrators had promised me a liberal compensation in case I succeeded, as well as a fair consideration of the improvements I had made to their dynamos and I hoped to realize a substantial sum. There were three administrators, whom I shall designate as A, B, and C for convenience. When I called on A, he told me that B had the say. This gentleman thought that only C could decide, and the latter was quite sure that A alone had the power to act. After several laps of this circulus viciosus, it dawned upon me that my reward was a castle in Spain.

The utter failure of my attempts to raise capital for development was another disappointment, and when Mr. Batchellor pressed me to go to America with a view of redesigning the Edison machines, I determined to try my fortunes in the Land of Golden Promise. But the chance was nearly missed. I liquefied my modest assets, secured accommodations and found myself at the railroad station as the train was pulling out. At that moment, I discovered that my money and tickets were gone. What to do was the question. Hercules had plenty of time to deliberate, but I had to decide while running alongside the train with opposite feelings surging in my brain like condenser oscillations. Resolve, helped by dexterity, won out in the nick of time and upon passing thru the usual experience, as trivial as unpleasant, I managed to embark for New York wtih the remnants of my belongings, some poems and articles I had written, and a package of calculations relating to solutions of an unsolvable integral and my flying machine. During the voyage I sat most of the time at the stern of the ship watching for an opportunity to save somebody from a watery grave, without the slightest thought of danger. Later, when I had absorbed some of the practical American sense, I shivered at the recollection and marvelled at my former folly. The meeting wtih Edison was a memorable event in my life. I was amazed at this wonderful man who, without early advantages and scientific training, had accomplished so much. I had studied a dozen languages, delved in literature and art, and had spent my best years in libraries reading all sorts of stuff that fell into my hands, from Newton's 'Principia' to the novels of Paul de Kock, and felt that most of my life had been squandered. But it did not take long before I recognized that it was the best thing I could have done. Within a few weeks I had won Edison's confidence, and it came about in this way.

The S.S. Oregon, the fastest passenger steamer at that time, had both of

its lighting machines disabled and its sailing was delayed. As the super-
structure had been built after their installation, it was impossible to remove
them from the hold. The predicament was a serious one and Edison was much an-
noyed. In the evening I took the necessary instruments with me and went
aboard the vessel where I stayed for the night. The dynamos were in bad
condition, having several short-circuits and breaks, but with the assistance
of the crew, I succeeded in putting them in good shape. At five o'clock in
the morning, when passing along Fifth Avenue on my way to the shop, I met
Edison with Batchellor and a few others, as they were returning home to
retire. 'Here is our Parisian running around at night,' he said. When I
told him that I was coming from the Oregon and had repaired both machines,
he looked at me in silence and walked away without another word. But when
he had gone some distance I heard him remark, 'Batchellor, this is a good
man.' And from that time on I had full freedom in directing the work. For
nearly a year my regular hours were from 10:30 A.M. until 5 o'clock the next
morning without a day's exception. Edison said to me, 'I have had many hard-
working assistants, but you take the cake.' During this period I designed
twenty-four different types of standard machines with short cores and uniform
pattern, which replaced the old ones. The Manager had promised me fifty
thousand dollars on the completion of this task, but it turned out to be
a practical joke. This gave me a painful shock and I resigned my position.

Immediately thereafter, some people approached me with the proposal of
forming an arc light company under my name, to which I agreed. Here finally,
was an opportunity to develop the motor, but when I broached the subject
to my new associates they said, 'No, we want the arc lamp. We don't care
for this alternating current of yours.' In 1886 my system of arc lighting
was perfected and adopted for factory and municipal lighting, and I was
free, but with no other possession than a beautifully engraved certificate
of stock of hypothetical value. Then followed a period of struggle in the
new medium for which I was not fitted, but the reward came in the end, and
in April, 1887, the TESLA Electric Co. was organized, providing a laboratory
and facilities. The motors I built there were exactly as I had imagined them.
I made no attempt to improve the design, but merely reproduced the pictures
as they appeared to my vision and the operation was always as I expected.

In the early part of 1888, an arrangement was made with the Westinghouse
Company for the manufacture of the motors on a large scale. But great
difficulties had still to be overcome. My system was based on the use of
low frequency currents and the Westinghouse experts had adopted 133 cycles
with the object of securing advantages in the transformation. They did not
want to depart from their standard forms of apparatus and my efforts had to
be concentrated upon adapting the motor to these conditions. Another necessity was to produce a motor capable of running efficiently at this frequency
on two wires, which was not an easy accomplishment.

At the close of 1889, however, my services in Pittsburg being no longer
essential, I returned to New York and resumed experimental work in a Laboratory
on Grand Street, where I began immediately the design of high-frequency machines.
The problems of construction in this unexplored field were novel and quite
peculiar, and I encountered many difficulties. I rejected the inductor type,
fearing that it might not yield perfect sine waves, which were so important
to resonant action. Had it not been for this, I could have saved myself a
great deal of labor. Another discouraging feature of the high-frequency
alternator seemed to be the inconstancy of speed which threatened to impose
serious limitations to its use. I had already noted in my demonstrations
before the American Institution of Electrical Engineers, that several times

the tune was lost, necessitating readjustment, and did not yet foresee what I discovered long afterwards,---a means of operating a machine of this kind at a speed constant to such a degree as not to vary more than a small fraction of one revolution between the extremes of load. From many other considerations, it appeared desirable to invent a simpler device for the production of electric oscillations.

In 1856, Lord Kelvin had exposed the theory of the condenser discharge, but no practical application of that important knowledge was made. I saw the possibilities and undertook the development of induction apparatus on this principle. My progress was so rapid as to enable me to exhibit at my lecture in 1891, a coil giving sparks of five inches. On that occasion I frankly told the engineers of a defect involved in the transformation by the new method, namely, the loss in the spark gap. Subsequent investigation showed that no matter what medium is employed,---be it air, hydrogen, mercury, vapor, oil, or a stream of electrons, the efficiency is the same. It is a law very much like the governing of the conversion of mechanical energy. We may drop a weight form a certain height vertically down, or carry it to the lower level along any devious path; it is immaterial insofar as the amount of work is concerned. Fortunately however, this drawback is not fatal, as by proper proportioning of the resonant, circuits an efficiency of 85 per cent is attainable. Since my early announcement of the invention, it has come into universal use and wrought a revolution in many departments, but a still greater future awaits it.

When in 1900 I obtained powerful discharges of 1,000 feet and flashed a current around the globe, I was reminded of the first tiny spark I observed in my Grand Street laboratory and was thrilled by sensations akin to those I felt when I discovered the rotating magnetic field.

As I review the events of my past life I realize how subtle are the influences that shape our destinies. An incident of my youth may serve to illustrate. One winter's day I managed to climb a steep mountain, in company with the other boys. The snow was quite deep and a warm southerly wind made it just suitable for our purpose. We amused ourselves by throwing balls which would roll down a certain distance, gathering more or less snow, and we tried to out do one another in this sport. Suddenly a ball was seen to go beyond the limit, swelling to enormous proportions until it became as big as a house and plunged thundering into the valley below with a force that made the ground tremble. I looked on spellbound incapable of understanding what had happened. For weeks afterward the picture of the avalanche was before my eyes and I wondered how anything so small could grow to such an immense size.

Ever since that time the magnification of feeble actions fascinated me, and when, years later, I took up the experimental study of mechanical and electrical resonance, I was keenly interested from the very start. Possibly, had it not been for that early powerful impression I might not have followed up the little spark I obtained with my coil and never developed my best invention, the true history of which I will tell.

Many technical men, very able in their special departments, but dominated by a pendantic spirit and near-sighted, have asserted that excepting the induction motor, I have given to the world little of practical use. This is a grievous mistake. A new idea must not be judged by its immediate results. My alternating system of power transmission came at a psychological moment, as a long sought answer to pressing industrial questions, and although considerable resistance had to be overcome and opposing interests reconciled, as usual, the commercial introduction could not be long delayed. Now, compare this situation with that confronting my turbines, for example. One should think that so simple and beautiful an invention, possessing many features of an ideal motor, should be adopted at once and, undoubtedly, it would uner similar conditions. But the prospective effect of the rotating field was not to render worthless existing machinery; on the contrary, it was to give it additional value. The system lent itself to new enterprise as well as to improvement of the old. My turbine is an advance of a character entirely different. It is a radical departure in the sense that its success would mean the abandonment of the antiquated types of prime movers on which billions of dollars have been spent. Under such circumstances, the progress must needs be slow and perhaps the greatest impediment is encountered in the prejudicial opinions created in the minds of experts by organized opposition.

Only the other day, I had a disheartening experience when I met my friend and former assistant, Charles F. Scott, now professor of Electric Engineering at Yale. I had not seen him for a long time and was glad to have an opportunity for a little chat at my office. Our conversation, naturally enough, drifted on my turbine and I became heated to a high degree. 'Scott,' I exclaimed, carried away by the vision of a glorious future, 'My turbine will scrap all the heat engines in the world.' Scott stroked his chin and looked away thoughtfully, as though making a mental calculation. 'That will make quite a pile of scrap,' he said, and left without another word!

These and other inventions of mine, however, were nothing more than steps forward in certain directions. In evolving them, I simply followed the inborn instinct to improve the present devices without any special thought of our far more imperative necessities. The 'Magnifying Transmitter' was the product of labors extending through years, having for their chief object, the solution of problems which are infinitely more important to mankind than mere industrial development.

If my memory serves me right, it was in November, 1890, that I performed a laboratory experiment which was one of the most extraordinary and spectacular ever recorded in the annuals of Science. In investigating the behaviour of high frequency currents, I had satisfied myself that an electric field of sufficient intensity could be produced in a room to light up electrodeless vacuum tubes. Accordingly, a transformer was built to test the theory and the first trial proved a marvelous success. It is difficult to appreciate what those strange phenomena meant at the time. We crave for new sensations, but soon become indifferent to them. The wonders of yesterday are today common occurrences. When my tubes were first publicly exhibited, they were viewed with amazement impossible to describe. From all parts of the world, I received urgent invitations and numerous honours and other flattering inducements were offered to me, which I declined. But in 1892 the demand became irresistible and I went to London where I delivered a lecture before the institution of Electrical Engineers.

It had been my intention to leave immediately for Paris in compliance with a similar obligation, but Sir James Dewar insisted on my appearing before the Royal Institution. I was a man of firm resolve, but succumbed easily to the forceful arguments of the great Scotchman. He pushed me into a chair and poured out half a glass of a wonderful brown fluid which sparkled in all sorts of iridescent colours and tasted like nectar. 'Now,' said he, 'you are sitting in Faraday's chair and you are enjoying whiskey he used to drink.' (Which did not interest me very much, as I had altered my opinion concerning strong drink). The next evening I gave a demonstration before the Royal Institution, at the termination of which, Lord Rayleigh addressed the audience and his generous words gave me the first start in these endeavors. I fled from London and later from Paris, to escape favors showered upon me, and journeyed to my home, where I passed through a most painful ordeal and illness.

Upon regaining my health, I began to formulate plans for the resumption of work in America. Up to that time I never realized that I possessed any particular gift of discovery, but Lord Rayleigh, whom I always considered as an ideal man of science, had said so and if that was the case, I felt that I should concentrate on some big idea.

At this time, as at many other times in the past, my thoughts turned towards my Mother's teaching. The gift of mental power comes from God, Divine Being, and if we concentrate our minds on that truth, we become in tune with this great power. My Mother had taught me to seek all truth in the Bible; therefore I devoted the next few months to the study of this work.

One day, as I was roaming in the mountains, I sought shelter from an approaching storm. The sky became overhung with heavy clouds, but somehow the rain was delayed until, all of a sudden, there was a lightning flash and a few moments after, a deluge. This observation set me thinking. It was manifest that the two phenomena were closely related, as cause and effect, and a little reflection led me to the conclusion that the electrical energy involved in the precipitation of the water was inconsiderable, the function of lightning being much like that of a sensitive trigger. Here was a stupendous possibility of achievement. If we could produce electric effects of the required quality, this whole planet and the conditions of existence on it could be transformed. The sun raises the water of the oceans and winds drive it to distant regions where it remains in a state of most delicate balance. If it were in our power to upset it when and wherever desired, this mighty life sustaining stream could be at will controlled. We could irrigate arid deserts, create lakes and rivers, and provide motive power in unlimited amounts. This would be the most efficient way of harnessing the sun to the uses of man. The consumation depended on our ability to develop electric forces of the order of those in nature.

It seemed a hopeless undertaking, but I made up my mind to try it and immediately on my return to the United States in the summer of 1892, after a short visit to my friends in Watford, England; work was begun which was to me all the more attractive, because a means of the same kind was necessary for the successful transmission of energy without wires.

At this time I made a further careful study of the Bible, and discovered the key in Revelation. The first gratifying result was obtained in the spring of the succeeding year, when I reached a tension of about 100,000,000 volts -- one hundred million volts--with my conical coil, which I figured was the voltage of a flash of lightning. Steady progress was made until the destruction of my laboratory by fire, in 1895, as may be judged from an article by T. C. Martin which appeared in the April number of the Century Magazine. This calamity set me back in many ways and most of that year had to be devoted to planning and reconstruction. However, as soon as circumstances permitted, I returned to the task.

Although I knew that higher electric-motive forces were attainable with apparatus of larger dimensions, I had an instinctive perception that the object could be accomplished by the proper design of a comparatively small and compact transformer. In carrying on tests with a secondary in the form of flat spiral, as illustrated in my patents, the absence of streamers surprised me, and it was not long before I discovered that this was due to the position of the turns and their mutual action. Profiting from this observation, I resorted to the use of a high tension conductor with turns of considerable diameter, sufficiently separated to keep down the distributed capacity, while at the same time preventing undue accumulation of the charge at any point. The application of this principle enabled me to produce pressures of over 100,000,000 volts, which was about the limit obtainable without risk of accident. A photograph of my transmitter built in my laboratory at Houston Street, was published in the Electrical Review of November, 1898.

In order to advance further along this line, I had to go into the open, and in the spring of 1899, having completed preparations for the erection of a wireless plant, I went to Colorado where I remained for more than one year. Here I introduced other improvements and refinements which made it possible to generate currents of any tension that may be desired. Those who are interested will find some information in regard to the experiments I conducted there in my article, 'The Problem of Increasing Human Energy,' in the Century Magazine of June 1900, to which I have referred on a previous occasion.

I will be quite explicit on the subject of my magnifying transformer so that it will be clearly understood. In the first place, it is a resonant transformer, with a secondary in which the parts, charged to a high potential, are of considerable area and arranged in space along ideal enveloping surfaces of very large radii of curvature, and at proper distances from one another, thereby insuring a small electric surface density everywhere, so that no leak can occur even if the conductor is bare. It is suitable for any frequency, from a few to many thousands of cycles per second, and can be used in the production of currents of tremendous volume and moderate pressure, or of smaller amperage and immense electromotive force. The maximum electric tension is merely dependent on the curvature of the surfaces on which the charged elements are situated and the area of the latter. Judging from my past experience there is no limit to the possible voltage developed; any amount is practicable. On the other hand, currents of many thousands of amperes may be obtained in the antenna. A plant of but very moderate dimensions is required for such performances. Theoretically, a terminal of less than 90 feet in diameter is sufficient to develop an electromotive force of that magnitude, while for antenna currents of from 2,000 -4,000 amperes at the usual frequencies, it need not be larger than 30 feet in diameter. In a more restricted meaning, this wireless transmitter is one in which the Hertzwave radiation is an entirely negligible quantity as compared with the whole energy, under which condition the damping factor is extremely small and an enormous charge is stored in the elevated capacity. Such a circuit may then be excited with impulses of any kind, even of low frequency and it will yield sinusoidel and continuous oscillations like those of an alternator. Taken in the narrowest significance of the term, however, it is a resonant transformer which, besides possessing these qualities, is accurately proportioned to fit the globe and its electrical constants and properties, by virtue of which design it becomes highly efficient and effective in the wireless transmission of energy. Distance is then ABSOLUTELY ELIMINATED, THERE BEING NO DIMINUATION IN THE INTENSITY of the transmitted impulses. It is even possible to make the actions increase with the distance from the plane, according to an exact mathematical law. This invention was one of a number comprised in my "World-System" of wireless transmission which I undertook to commercialize on my return to New York in 1900.

As to the immediate purposes of my enterprise, they were clearly outlined in a technical statement of that period from which I quote, "The world system has resulted from a combination of several original discoveryes made by the inventor in the course of long continued research and experimentation. It makes possible not only the instantaneous and precise wireless transmission of any kind of signals, messages or characters, to all parts of the world, but also the inter-connection of the existing telegraph, telephone, and other signal stations without any change in their present equipment. By its means, for instance, a telephone subscriber here may call up and talk to any other subscriber on the Earth. An inexpensive receiver, not bigger than a watch, will enable him to listen anywhere, on land or sea, to a speech delivered or music played in some other place, however distant."

These examples are cited merely to give an idea of the possibilities of this great scientific advance, which annihilates distance and makes that perfect natural conductor, the Earth, available for all the innumerable purposes which human ingenuity has found for a line-wire. One far-reaching result·of this is that  any device capable of being operated thru one or more wires (at a distance obviously restricted) can likewise be actuated, without artificial conductors and with the same facility and accuracy, at distances to which there are no limits other than those imposed by the physical dimensions of the earth. Thus, not only will entirely new fields for commercial exploitation be opened up by this ideal method of transmission, but the old ones vastly extended. The World System is based on the application of the following important inventions and discoveries:

1) The Tesla Transformer: This apparatus is in the production of elec-

trical vibrations as revolutionary as gunpowder was in warfare. Currents many times stronger than any ever generated in the usual ways and sparks over one hundred feet long, have been produced by the inventor with an instrument of this kind.

2) The Magnifying Transmitter: This is Tesla's best invention, a peculiar transformer specially adapted to excite the Earth, which is in the transmission of electrical energy when the telescope is in astronomical observation. By the use of this marvelous device, he has already set up electrical movements of greater intensity than those of lightning and passed a current, sufficient to light more than two hundred incandescent lamps, around the Earth.

3) The Tesla Wireless System: This system comprises a number of improvements and is the only means known for transmitting economically electrical energy to a distance without wires. Careful tests and measurements in connection with an experimental station of great activity, erected by the inventor in Colorado, have demonstrated that power in any desired amount can be conveyed, clear across the Globe if necessary, with a loss not exceeding a few per cent.

4) The Art of Individualization: This invention of Tesla is to primitive Tuning, what refined language is to unarticulated expression. It makes possible the transmission of signals or messages absolutely secret and exclusive both in the active and passive aspect, that is, noninterfering as well as non-interferable. Each signal is like an individual of unmistakable identity and there is virtually no limit to the number of stations or instruments which can be simultaneously operated without the slightest mutual disturbance.

5) The Terrestial Stationary Waves: This wonderful discovery, popularly explained, means that the Earth is responsive to electrical vibrations of definite pitch, just as a tuning fork to certain waves of sound. These particular electrical vibrations, capable of powerfully exciting the Globe, lend themselves to innumerable uses of great importance commercially and in many other respects. The 'first World System' power plant can be put in operation in nine months. With this power plant, it will be practicable to attain electrical activities up to ten million horse-power and it is designed to serve for as many technical achievements as are possible without due expense. Among these are the following:

1) The inter-connection of existing telegraph exchanges or offices all over the world;
2) The establishment of a secret and non-interferable government telegraph service;
3) The inter-connection of all present telephone exchanges or offices on the Globe;
4) The universal distribution of general news by telegraph or telephone, in connection with the Press;
5) The establishment of such a 'World System' of intelligence transmission for exclusive private use;
6) The inter-connection and operation of all stock tickers of the world;
7) The establishment of a World system--of musical distribution, etc.;
8) The universal registration of time by cheap clocks indicating the hour with astronomical precision and requiring no attention whatever;
9) The world transmission of typed or hand-written characters, letters, checks, etc.;
10) The establishment of a universal marine service enabling the navigators of all ships to steer perfectly without compass, to determine the exact location, hour and speed; to prevent collisions and disasters, etc.;

11) The inauguration of a system of world printing on land and sea;
12) The world reproduction of photographic pictures and all kinds of drawings or records...."

I also proposed to make demonstration in the wireless transmission of po-war on a small scale, but sufficient to carry conviction. Besides these, I referred to other and incomparably more important applications of my discoveries which will be disclosed at some future date. A plant was built on Long Island with a tower 187 feet high, having a spherical terminal about 68 feet in diameter. These dimensions were adequate for the transmission of virtually any amount of energy. Originally, only from 200 to 300 K.W. were provided, but I intended to employ later several thousand horsepower. The transmitter was to emit a wave-complex of special characteristics and I had devised a unique method of telephonic control of any amount of energy. The tower was destroyed two years ago (1917) but my projects are being developed and another one, improved in some features will be constructed.

On this occasion I would contradict the widely circulated report that the structure was demolished by the Government, which owing to war conditions, might have created prejudice in the minds of those who may not know that the papers, which thirty years ago conferred upon me the honour of American citizenship, are always kept in a safe, while my orders, diplomas, degrees, gold medals and other distinctions are packed away in old trunks. If this report had a foundation, I would have been refunded a large sum of money which I expended in the construction of the tower. On the contrary, it was in the interest of the Government to preserve it, particularly as it would have made possible, to mention just one valuable result, the location of a submarine in any part of the world. My plant, services, and all my improvements have always been at the disposal of the officials and ever since the outbreak of the European conflict, I have been working at a sacrifice on several inventions of mine relating to aerial navigation, ship propulsion and wireless transmission, which are of the greatest importance to the country. Those who are well informed know that my ideas have revolutionized the industries of the United States and I am not aware that there lives an inventor who has been, in this respect, as fortunate as myself,--especially as regards the use of his improvements in the war.

I have refrained from publicly expressing myself on this subject before, as it seemed improper to dwell on personal matters while all the world was in dire trouble. I would add further, in view of various rumors which have reached me, that Mr. J. Pierpont Morgan did not interest himself with me in a business way, but in the same large spirit in which he has assisted many other pioneers. He carried out his generous promise to the letter and it would have been most unreasonable to expect from him anything more. He had the highest regard for my attainments and gave me every evidence of his complete faith in my ability to ultimately achieve what I had set out to do. I am unwilling to accord to some small-minded and jealous individuals the satisfaction of having thwarted my efforts. These men are to me nothing more than microbes of a nasty disease. My project was retarded by laws of nature. The world was not prepared for it. It was too far ahead of time, but the same laws will prevail in the end and make it a triumphal success.

No subject to which I have ever devoted myself has called for such concentration of mind, and strained to so dangerous a degree the finest fibres of my brain, as the system of which the Magnifying transmitter is the foundation. I put all the intensity and vigor of youth in the development of the rotating field discoveries, but those early labors were of a different character. Although strenuous in the extreme, they did not involve that keen and exhausting discernment which had to be exercised in attacking the many problems of the wireless.

Despite my rare physical endurance at that period, the abused nerves finally rebelled and I suffered a complete collapse, just as the consumation of the long and difficult task was almost in sight. Without doubt I would have paid a greater penalty later, and very likely my career would have been prematurely terminated, had not providence equipped me with a safety device, which seemed to improve with advancing years and unfailingly comes to play when my forces are at an end. So long as it operates I am safe from danger, due to overwork, which threatens other inventors, and incidentally, I need no vacations which are indispensible to most people. When I am all but used up, I simply do as the darkies who "naturally fall asleep while white folks worry."

To venture a theory out of my sphere, the body probably accumulates little by little a definite quantity of some toxic agent and I sink into a nearly lethargic state which lasts half an hour to the minute. Upon awakening I have the sensation as though the events immediately preceding had occurred very long ago, and if I attempt to continue the interrupted train of thought I feel veritable mental nausea. Involuntarily, I then turn to other work and am surprised at the freshness of the mind and ease with which I overcome obstacles that had baffled me before. After weeks or months, my passion for the temporarily abandoned invention returns and I invariably find answers to all the vexing questions, with scarcely any effort. In this connection, I will tell of an extraordinary experience which may be of interest to students of psychology.

I had produced a striking phenomenon with my grounded transmitter and was endeavoring to ascertain its true significance in relation to the currents propagated through the earth. It seemed a hopeless undertaking, and for more than a year I worked unremittingly, but in vain. This profound study so entirely absorbed me, that I became forgetful of everything else, even of my undermined health. At last, as I was at the point of breaking down, nature applied the preservative inducing lethal sleep. Regaining my senses, I realized with consternation that I was unable to visualize scenes from my life except those of infancy, the very first ones that had entered my consciousness. curiously enough, these appeared before my vision with startling distinctness and afforded me welcome relief. Night after night, when retiring, I would think of them and more and more of my previous existence was revealed. The image of my mother was always the principal figure in the spectacle that slowly unfolded, and a consuming desire to see her again gradually took possession of me. This feeling grew so strong that I resolved to drop all work and satisfy my longing, but I found it too hard to break away from the laboratory, and several months elapsed during which I had succeeded in reviving all the impressions of my past life, up to the spring of 1892. In the next picture that came out of the mist of oblivion, I saw myself at the Hotel de la Paix in Paris, just coming to from one of my peculiar sleeping spells, which had been caused by prolonged exertion of the brain.  Imagine the pain and distress I felt, when it flashed upon my mind that a dispatch was handed to me at that very moment, bearing the sad news that my mother was dying.  I remembered how I made the long journey home without an hour of rest and how she passed away after weeks of agony.

It was especially remarkable that during all this period of partially obliterated memory, I was fully alive to everything touching on the subject of my research.  I could recall the smallest detail and the least insignificant observations in my experiments and even recite pages of text and complex mathematical formulae.

My belief is firm in a law of compensation.  The true rewards are ever in proportion to the labor and sacrifices made.  This is one of the reasons why I feel certain that of all my inventions, the magnifying Transmitter will prove most important and valuable to future generations.  I am prompted to this prediction, not so much by thoughts of the commercial and industrial revolution which it will surely bring about, but of the humanitation consequences of the many achievements it makes possible.  Considerations of mere utility weight little in the balance against the higher benefits of civilization.  We are confronted with portentious problems which can not be solved just by providing for our material existence, however abundantly.  On the contrary, progress in this direction is fraught with hazards and perils not less menacing than those born from want and suffering.  If we were to release the energy of atoms or discover some other way of developing cheap and unlimited power at any point on the globe, this accomplishment, instead of being a blessing, might bring disaster to mankind in giving rise to dissension and anarchy, which would ultimately result in the enthronement of the hated regime of force.  The greatest good will come from technical improvements tending to unification and harmony, and my wireless transmitter is preeminently such.  By its means, the human voice and likeness will be reproduced everywhere and factories driven thousands of miles from waterfalls furnishing the power.  Aerial machines will be propelled around the earth without a stop and the sun's energy controlled to create lakes and rivers for motive purposes and transformation of arid deserts into fertile land.  Its introduction for telegraphic, telephonic and similar uses, will automatically cut out the statics and all other interferences which at present, impose narrow limits to the application of the wireless.  This is a timely topic on which a few words might not be amiss.

During the past decade a number of people have arrogantly claimed that they had succeeded in doing away with this impediment.  I have carefully examined all of the arrangements described and tested most of them long before they were publicly disclosed, but the finding was uniformly negative.  Recent official statement from the U.S. Navy may, perhaps, have taught some beguilable news editors how to appraise these announcements at their real worth.  As a rule, the attempts are based on theories so fallacious, that whenever they come to my notice, I can not help thinking in a light vein.  Quite recently a new discovery was heralded, with a deafening flourish of trumpets, but it proved another case of a mountain bringing forth a mouse.  This reminds me of an exciting incident which took place years ago, when I was conducting my experiments with currents of high frequency.

Steve Brodie had just jumped off the Brooklyn Bridge.  The feat has been vulgarized since by imitators, but the first report electrified New York.  I was very impressionable then and frequently spoke of the daring printer.  On a hot afternoon I felt the necessity of refreshing myself and stepped into

one of the popular thirty thousand institutions of this great city, where a
delicious twelve per cent beverage was served, which can now be had only by
making a trip to the poor and devastated countries of Europe. The attendance
was large and not over-distinguished and a matter was discussed which gave me
an admirable opening for the careless remark, 'This is what I said when I
jumped off the bridge.' No sooner had I uttered these words, than I felt like
the companion of Timothens, in the poem of Schiller. In an instant there was
pandomonium and a dozen voices cried, 'It is Brodie!' I threw a quarter on
the counter and bolted for the door, but the crowd was at my heels with yells,
---'Stop, Steeve!', which must have been misunderstood, for many persons tried
to hold me up as I ran frantically for my haven of refuge. By darting around
corners I fortunately managed, through the medium of a fire escape, to reach
the laboratory, where I threw off my coat, camouflaged myself as a hard-work-
ing blacksmith and started the forge. But these precautions proved unneces-
sary, as I had eluded my pursuers. For many years afterward, at night, when
imagination turns into spectres the trifling troubles of the day, I often
thought, as I tossed on the bed, what my fate would have been, had the mob
caught me and found out that I was not Steve Brodie!

Now the engineer who lately gave an account before a technical body of
a novel remedy against statics based on a 'heretofore unknown law of nature,'
seems to have been as reckless as myself when he contended that these disturbances propagate up and down, while those of a transmitter proceed along
the earth. It would mean that a condenser as this globe, with its gaseous envelope, could be charged and discharged in a manner quite contrary to the
fundamental teachings propounded in every elemental text book of physics.
Such a supposition would have been condemned as erroneous, even in Franklin's
time, for the facts bearing on this were then well-known and the identity
between atmospheric electricity and that developed by machines was fully
established. Obviously, natural and artificial disturbances propagate through
the earth and the air in exactly the same way, and both set up electromotive forces in the horizontal, as well as vertical sense. Interference
can not be overcome by any such methods as were proposed. The truth is this:
In the air the potential increases at the rate of about fifty volts per foot
of elevation, owing to which there may be a difference of pressure amounting
to twenty, or even forty thousand volts between the upper and lower ends of
the antenna. The masses of the charged atmosphere are constantly in motion
and give up electricity to the conductor, not continuously, but rather dis-
ruptively, this producing a grinding noise in a sensitive telephonic receiver.
The higher the terminal and the greater the space encompast by the wires, the
more pronounced is the effect, but it must be understood that it is purely
local and has little to do with the real trouble.

In 1900, while perfecting my wireless system, one form of apparatus
comprised four antennae. These were carefully calibrated in the same
frequency and connected in multiple with the object of magnifying the action
in receiving from any direction. When I desired to ascertain the origin of
the transmitted impulses, each diagonally situated pair was put in series with
a primary coil energizing the detector circuit. In the former case, the sound
was loud in the telephone; in the latter it ceased, as expected,--the two
antennae neutralizing each other, but the true statics manifested themselves
in both instances and I had to devise special preventives embodying different
principles. By employing receivers connected to two points of the ground, as
suggested by me long ago, this trouble caused by the charged air, which is very
serious in the structures as now built, is nullified and besides, the liabil-
ity of all kinds of interference is reduced to about one-half because of the
directional character of the circuit. This was perfectly self-evident, but

40

came as a revelation to some simple-minded wireless folks whose experience was confined to forms of apparatus that could have been improved with an axe, and they have been disposing of the bear's skin before killing him. If it were true that strays performed such antics, it would be easy to get rid of them by receiving without aerials. But, as a matter of fact, a wire buried in the ground which, conforming to this view, should be absolutely immune, is more susceptible to certain extraneous impulses than one placed vertically in the air. To state it fairly, a slight progress has been made, but not by virtue of any particular method or device. It was achieved simply by discerning the enormous structures, which are bad enough for transmission but wholly unsuitable for reception and adopting a more appropriate type of receiver. As I have said before, to dispose of this difficulty for good, a radical change must be made in the system and the sooner this is done the better.

It would be calamitus, indeed, if at this time when the art is in its infancy and the vast majority, not excepting even experts, have no conception of its ultimate possibilities, a measure would be rushed through the legislature making it a government monopoly. This was proposed a few weeks ago by Secretary Daniels and no doubt that distinguished official has made his appeal to the Senate and House of Representatives with sincere conviction. But universal evidence unmistakably shows that the best results are always obtained in healthful commercial competition. There are, however, exceptional reasons why wireless should be given the fullest freedom of development. In the first place, it offers prospects immeasurably greater and more vital to betterment of human life than any other invention or discovery in the history of man. Then again, it must be understood that this wonderful art has been, in its entirety, evolved here and can be called 'American' with more right and propriety than the telephone, the incandescent lamp or the aeroplane.

Enterprising press agents and stock jobbers have been so successful in spreading misinformation, that even so excellent a periodical as the Scientific American, accords the chief credit to a foreign country. The Germans, of course, gave us the Hertz-waves and the Russian, English, French and Italian experts were quick in using them for signalling purposes. It was an obvious application of the new agent and accomplished with the old classical and unimproved induction coil, scarcely anything more than another kind of heliography. The radius of transmission was very limited, the result attained of little value, and the Hertz oscillations, as a means for conveying intelligence, could have been advantageously replaced by sound-waves, which I advocated in 1891. Moreover, all of these attempts were made three years after the basic principles of the wireless system, which is universally employed today, and its potent instrumentalities had been clearly described and developed in America.

No trace of those Hertzian appliances and methods remains today. We have proceeded in the very opposite direction and what has been done is the product of the brains and efforts of citizens of this country. The fundamental patents have expired and the opportunities are open to all. The chief argument of the Secretary is based on interference. According to his statement, reported in the New York Herald of July 29th, signals from a powerful station can be intercepted in every village in the world. In view of this fact, which was demonstrated in my experiments of 1900, it would be of little use to impose restrictions in the United States.

As throwing light on this point, I may mention that only recently an odd looking gentleman called on me with the object of enlisting my services in the construction of world transmitters in some distant land. 'We have no money,'

he said, 'but carloads of solid gold, and we will give you a liberal amount.'
I told him that I wanted to see first what will be done with my inventions in
America, and this ended the interview.  But I am satisfied that some dark forces are at work, and as time goes on the maintenance of continuous communication will be rendered more difficult.  The only remedy is a system immune
against interruption.  It has been perfected, it exists, and all that is necessary is to put it in operation.

The terrible conflict is still uppermost in the minds and perhaps the
greatest importance will be attached to the magnifying Transmitter as a machine for attack and defense, more particularly in connection with TELAUTAMATICS.
This invention is a logical outcome of observations begun in my boyhood and
continued thruout my life.  When the first results were published, the Electrical Review stated editorially that it would become one of the 'most potent
factors in the advance and civilization of mankind.'  The time is not distant
when this prediction will be fulfilled.  In 1898 and 1900, it was offered by
me to the Government and might have been adopted, were I one of those who
would go to Alexander's shepherd when they want a favor from Alexander!

At that time I really thought that it would abolish war, because of its
unlimited destructiveness and exclusion of the personal element of combat.
But while I have not lost faith in its potentialities, my views have changed
since.  War can not be avoided until the physical cause for its recurrence is
removed and this, in the last analysis, is the vast extent of the planet on
which we live.  Only thru annihilation of distance in every respect, as the
conveyance of intelligence, transport of passengers and supplies and transmission of energy will conditions be brought about some day, insuring perman-
ency of friendly relations.  What we now want most is closer contact and better understanding between individuals and communities all over the earth and
the elimination of that fanatic devotion to exalted ideals of national egoism
and pride, which is always prone to plunge the world into primeval barbarism
and strife.  No league or parliamentary act of any kind will ever prevent such
a calamity.  These are only new devices for putting the weak at the mercy of
the strong.

I have expressed myself in this regard fourteen years ago, when a combination of a few leading governments, a sort of Holy alliance, was advocated by
the late Andrew Carnegie, who may be fairly considered as the father of this
idea, having given to it more publicity and impetus than anybody else prior to
the efforts of the President.  While it can not be denied that such aspects
might be of material advantage to some less fortunate peoples, it can not attain the chief objective sought.  Peace can only come as a natural consequence
of universal enlightenment and merging of races, and we are still far from this
blissful realization, because few indeed, will admit the reality--that God made
man in His image--in which case all earth men are alike.  There is in fact but
one race, of many colours.  Christ is but one person, yet he is of all people,
so why do some people think themselves better than some other people?

As I view the world of today, in the light of the gigantic struggle we
have witnessed, I am filled with conviction that the interests of humanity
would be best served if the United States remained true to its traditions,
true to God whom it pretends to believe, and kept out of "entangling alliances."
Situated as it is, geographically remote from the theaters of impending con-
flicts, without incentive to territorial aggrandisement, with inexhaustible
resources and immense population thoroughly imbued with the spirit of liberty
and right, this country is placed in a unique and privileged position.  It is

42

thus able to exert, independently, its collossal strength and moral force to the benefit of all, more judiciously and effectively, than as a member of a league.

I have dwelt on the circumstances of my early life and told of an affliction which compelled me to unremitting exercise of imagination and self-observation. This mental activity, at first involuntary under the pressure of illness and suffering, gradually became second nature and led me finally to recognise that I was but an automaton devoid of free will in thought and action and merely responsive to the forces of the environment. Our bodies are of such complexity of structure, the motions we perform are so numerous and involved and the external impressions on our sense organs to such a degree delicate and elusive, that it is hard for the average person to grasp this fact. Yet nothing is more convincing to the trained investigator than the mechanistic theory of life which had been, in a measure, understood and propounded by Descartes three hundred years ago. In his time many important functions of our organisms were unknown and especially with respect to the nature of light and the construction and operation of the eye, philosophers were in the dark.

In recent years the progress of scientific research in these fields has been such as to leave no room for a doubt in regard to this view on which many works have been published. One of its ablest and most eloquent exponents is, perhaps, Felix le Dantec, formerly assistant of Pasteur. Prof. Jacques Loeb has performed remarkable experiments in heliotropism, clearly establishing the controlling power of light in lower forms of organisms and his latest book, "Forced Movements," is revelatory. But while men of science accept this theory simply as any other that is recognized, to me it is a truth which I hourly demonstrate by every act and thought of mine. The consciousness of the external impression prompting me to any kind of exertion,--physical or mental, is ever present in my mind. Only on very rare occasions, when I was in a state of exceptional concentration, have I found difficulty in locating the original impulse. The by far greater number of human beings are never aware of what is passing around and within them and millions fall victims of disease and die prematurely just on this account. The commonest, every-day occurrences appear to them mysterious and inexplicable. One may feel a sudden wave of sadness and rack his brain for an explanation, when he might have noticed that it was caused by a cloud cutting off the rays of the sun. He may see the image of a friend dear to him under conditions which he construes as very peculiar, when only shortly before he has passed him in the street or seen his photograph somewhere. When he loses a collar button, he fusses and swears for an hour, being unable to visualize his previous actions and locate the object directly. Deficient observation is merely a form of ignorance and responsible for the many morbid notions and foolish ideas prevailing. There is not more than one out of every ten persons who does not believe in telepathy and other psychic manifestations, spiritualism and communion with the dead, and who would refuse to listen to willing or unwilling decievers?

Just to illustrate how deeply rooted this tendency has become even among the clear-headed American population, I may mention a comical incident. Shortly before the war, when the exhibition of my turbines in this city elicited widespread comment in the technical papers, I anticipated that there would be a scramble among manufacturers to get hold of the invention and I had particular designs on that man from Detroit who has an uncanny faculty for accumulating millions. So confident was I, that he would turn up some day, that I declared this as certain to my secretary and assistants. Sure enough, one fine morning a body of engineers from the Ford Motor Company presented themselves with the request of discussing with me an important project. "Didn't I tell you?," I remarked triumphantly to my employees, and one of them said, "You are amazing, Mr. Tesla. Everything comes out exactly as you predict."

As soon as these hard-headed men were seated, I of course, immediately began to extol the wonderful features of my turbine, when the spokesman interrupted me and said, "We know all about this, but we are on a special errand. We have formed a psychological society for the investigation of psychic phenomena and we want you to join us in this undertaking." I suppose these engineers never knew how near they came to being fired out of my office.

Ever since I was told by some of the greatest men of the time, leaders in science whose names are immortal, that I am possessed of an unusual mind, I bent all my thinking faculties on the solution of great problems regardless of sacrifice. For many years I endeavored to solve the enigma of death, and watched eagerly for every kind of spiritual indication. But only once in the course of my existence have I had an experience which momentarily impressed me as supernatural. It was at the time of my mother's death.

I had become completely exhausted by pain and long vigilance, and one night was carried to a building about two blocks from our home. As I lay helpless there, I thought that if my mother died while I was away from her bedside, she would surely give me a sign. Two or three months before, I was in London in company with my late friend, Sir William Crookes, when spiritualism was discussed and I was under the full sway of these thoughts. I might not have paid attention to other men, but was susceptible to his arguments as it was his epochal work on radiant matter, which I had read as a student, that made me embrace the electrical career. I reflected that the conditions for a look into the beyond were most favorable, for my mother was a woman of genius and particularly excelling in the powers of intuition. During the whole night every fiber in my brain was strained in expectancy, but nothing happened until early in the morning, when I fell in a sleep, or perhaps a swoon, and saw a cloud carrying angelic figures of marvelous beauty, one of whom gazed upon me lovingly and gradually assumed the features of my mother. The appearance slowly floated across the room and vanished, and I was awakened by an indescribably sweet song of many voices. In that instant a certitude, which no words can express, came upon me that my mother had just died. And that was true. I was unable to understand the tremendous weight of the painful knowledge I received in advance, and wrote a letter to Sir William Crookes while still under the domination of these impressions and in poor bodily health. When I recovered, I sought for a long time the external cause of this strange manifestation and, to my great relief, I succeeded after many months of fruitless effort.

I had seen the painting of a celebrated artist, representing allegorically one of the seasons in the form of a cloud with a group of angels which seemed to actually float in the air, and this had struck me forcefully. It was exactly the same that appeared in my dream, with the exception of my mother's likeness. The music came from the choir in the church nearby at the early mass of Easter morning, explaining everything satisfactorily in conformity with scientific facts.

This occurred long ago, and I have never had the faintest reason since to change my views on psychical and spiritual phenomena, for which there is no foundation. The belief in these is the natural outgrowth of intellectual development. Religious dogmas are no longer accepted in their orthodox meaning, but every individual clings to faith in a supreme power of some kind.

We all must have an ideal to govern our conduct and insure contentment, but it is immaterial whether it be one of creed, art, science, or anything else, so long as it fulfills the function of a dematerialising force. It is essential to the peaceful existence of humanity as a whole that one common conception should prevail. While I have failed to obtain any evidence in support of the contentions of psychologists and spiritualists, I have proved to my complete satisfaction the automatism of life, not only through continuous observations of individual actions, but even more conclusively through certain generalizations. These amount to a discovery which I consider of the greatest moment to human society, and on which I shall briefly dwell.

I got the first inkling of this astonishing truth when I was still a very young man, but for many years I interpreted what I noted simply as coincidences Namely, whenever either myself or a person to whom I was attached, or a cause to which I was devoted, was hurt by others in a particular way, which might be best popularly characterized as the most unfair imaginable, I experienced a singular and undefinable pain which, for the want of a better term, I have qualified as "cosmic" and shortly therafter, and invariably, those who had inflicted it came to grief. After many such cases I confided this to a number of friends, who had the opportunity to convince themselves of the theory of which I have gradually formulated and which may be stated in the following few words: Our bodies are of similar construction and exposed to the same external forces. This results in likeness of response and concordance of the general activities on which all our social and other rules and laws are based. We are automata entirely controlled by the forces of the medium, being tossed about like corks on the surface of the water, but mistaking the resultant of the impulses from the outside for the free will. The movements and other actions we perform are always life preservative and tho seemingly quite independent from one another, we are connected by invisible links. So long as the organism is in perfect order, it responds accurately to the agents that prompt it, but the moment that there is some derangement in any individual, his self-preservative power is impaired.

Everybody understands, of course, that if one becomes deaf, has his eyes weakened, or his limbs injured, the chances for his continued existence are lessened. But this is also true, and perhaps more so, of certain defects in the brain which deprives the automaton, more or less, of that vital quality and cause it to rush into destruction. A very sensitive and observant being, with his highly developed mechanism all intect, and acting with precision in obedience to the changing conditions of the environment, is endowed with a transcending mechanical sense, enabling him to evade perils too subtle to be directly perceived. When he comes in contact with others whose controlling organs are radically faulty, that sense asserts itself and he feels the "cosmic" pain.

The truth of this has been borne out in hundreds of instances and I am inviting other students of nature to devote attention to this subject, believing that thru combined and systematic effort, results of incalculable value to the world will be attained. The idea of constructing an automaton, to bear out my theory, presented itself to me early, but I did not begin active work until 1895, when I started my wireless investigations. During the succeeding two or three years, a number of automatic mechanisms, to be actuated from a distance, were constructed by me and exhibited to visitors in my laboratory.

In 1896, however, I designed a complete machine capable of a multitude of operations, but the consumation of my labors was delayed until late in 1897.

This machine was illustrated and described in my article in the Century Magazine of June, 1900; and other periodicals of that time and when first shown in the beginning of 1898, it created a sensation such as no other invention of mine has ever produced. In November, 1898, a basic patent on the novel art was granted to me, but only after the Examiner-in-Chief had come to New York and witnessed the performance, for what I claimed seemed unbelievable. I remember that when later I called on an official in Washington, with a view of offering the invention to the Government, he burst out in laughter upon my telling him what I had accomplished. Nobody thought then that there was the faintest prospect of perfecting such a device. It is unfortunate that in this patent, following the advice of my attorneys, I indicated the control as being affected thru the medium of a single circuit and a well-known form of detector, for the reason that I had not yet secured protection on my methods and apparatus for individualization. As a matter of fact, my boats were controlled thru the joint action of several circuits and interference of every kind was excluded.

Most generally, I employed receiving circuits in the form of loops, including condensers, because the discharges of my high-tension transmitter ionised the air in the (laboratory) so that even a very small aerial would draw electricity from the surrounding atmosphere for hours.

Just to give an idea, I found, for instance, that a bulb 12 inches in diameter, highly exhausted, and with one single terminal to which a short wire was attached, would deliver well on to one thousand successive flashes before all charge of the air in the laboratory was neutralised. The loop form of receiver was not sensitive to such a disturbance and it is curious to note that it is becoming popular at this late date. In reality, it collects much less energy than the aerials or a long gounded wire, but it so happens that it does away with a number of defects inherent to the present wireless devices.

In demonstrating my invention before audiences, the visitors were requested to ask questions, however involved, and the automaton would answer them by signs. This was considered magic at the time, but was extremely simple, for it was myself who gave the replies by means of the device.

At the same period, another larger tetautomatic boat was constructed, a photograph of which was shown in the October 1919 number of the Electrical Experimenter. It was controlled by loops, having several turns placed in the hull, which was made entirely water tight and capable of submergence. The apparatus was similar to that used in the first with the exception of certain special features I introduced as, for example, incandescent lamps which afforded a visible evidence of the proper functioning of the machine. These automata, controlled within the range of vision of the operator, were, however, the first and rather crude steps in the evolution of the art of Telautomatics as I had conceived it.

The next logical improvement was its application to automatic mechanisms beyond the limits of vision and at great distances from the center of control, and I have ever since advocated their employemnt as instruments of warfare in preference to guns. The importance of this now seems to be recognized, if I am to judge from casual announcements thru the press, of achievements which are said to be extraordinary but contain no merit of novelty, whatever. In an imperfect manner it is practicable, with the existing wireless plants, to launch an aeroplane, have it follow a certain approximate course, and perform some operation at a distance of many hundreds of miles. A machine of this kind can also be mechanically controlled in several ways and I have no doubt that it may prove of some usefulness in war. But there are to my best knowledge, no instrumentalities in existence today with which such an object could be accomplished in a precise manner. I have devoted years of study to this matter and have evolved means, making such and greater wonders easily realizable.

As stated on a previous occasion, when I was a student at college I conceived a flying machine quite unlike the present ones. The underlying principle was sound, but could not be carried into practice for want of a prime-mover of sufficiently great activity. In recent years I have successfully solved this problem and am now planning aerial machines devoid of sustaining planes, ailerons, propellers and other external attachments, which will be capable of immense speeds and are very likely to furnish powerful arguments for peace in the near future. Such a machine, sustained and propelled entirely by reaction, is shown on one of the pages of my lectures, and is supposed to be controlled either mechanically, or by wireless energy. By installing proper plants, it will be practicable to project a missile of this kind into the air and drop it almost on the very spot designated, which may be thousands of miles away.

But we are not going to stop at this. Telautomats will be ultimately produced, capable of acting as if possessed of their own intelligence, and their advent will create a revolution. As early as 1898, I proposed to representatives of a large manufacturing concern the construction and public exhibition of an automobile carriage which, left to itself, would perform a great variety of operations involving something akin to judgement. But my proposal was deemed chimerical at that time and nothing came of it.

At present, many of the ablest minds are trying to devise expedients for preventing a repetition of the awful conflict which is only theoretically ended and the duration and main issues of which I have correctly predicted in an article printed in the SUN of December 20, 1914. The proposed League is not a remedy but, on the contrary, in the opinion of a number of competent men, may bring about results just the opposite.

It is particularly regrettable that a punitive policy was adopted in framing the terms of peace, because a few years hence, it will be possible for nations to fight without armies, ships or guns, by weapons far more terrible, to the destructive action and range of which there is virtually no limit. Any city, at a distance, whatsoever, from the enemy, can by destroyed by him and no power on earth can stop him from doing so. If we want to avert an impending calamity and a state of things which may transform this globe into an inferno, we should push the development of flying machines and wireless transmission of energy without an instant's delay and with all the power and resources of the nation.

# THE WALL OF LIGHT

## Chapter 1

In relating this account of the landings of a large spaceship on my property at Lac Beauport, of my strange experience in meeting with people who claimed they were from Venus and what I learned about life on their planet, I would like to emphasize that I consider myself of little importance in this story. If my name is known at all, it is due to my long friendship with Nikola Tesla and an intimate knowledge of his great work for mankind. Perhaps I may be excused if I say that it affords me a certain amount of amused satisfaction to realize that I am now probably the last living person who knew and loved Tesla, but in all humility, I am aware that it was only because Tesla left me some of his ideas to develop that I was thus able to meet these people from Venus who claimed Tesla as one of their own.

Due to the fact that my story covers several visits of the Venusian spaceship, I am, for space reasons, condensing its details into one account and will therefore leave out dates. It is sufficient to say that the first visit was in Spring, 1941, with continued landings about every two years until 1961, which, to date, included the last landing. These landings took place on my 100-acre property in the hollow of a large meadow formed by the sloping mountainside at the back and the rise of ground at the front.

It was on a spring morning of 1941 that I was standing near my workshop with my son, Humphrey. We were discussing some matter relating to electrical waves when suddenly Humphrey looked up and exclaimed: "There's something wrong with the sun!" I looked to the east and gasped in astonishment. Exactly in the center of the golden disc there was a round black spot about one-quarter the apparent diameter of the sun. It was too big to be a sunspot and besides, it was moving. As we watched, it crept slowly to the upper edge of the sun and in about 10 minutes had left the solar disc when it simply vanished from sight. We saw nothing more of it that day.

I went to bed early that night but could not sleep. An oppressive sense of something strange impending descended on me like a pall. Finally, I arose and dressed. I went outside and looked up at the sky but all I could see were the stars sprkling in full brilliancy. I returned to the house and settled down to read - but not for long, for suddenly the alarm signal on the Tesla Scope rang shrilly. I ran outside and at first saw nothing except the sparkling stars. Then I noticed something queer toward the mountain. It appeared to be darker than usual. It was indeed, for some huge object seemed to cover most of the mountain! I began to walk toward it and as I came near to our barn, I was suddenly confronted by two persons.

Both men were nearly 6 feet tall and in the brilliant starlight I could discern their bright blue eyes and golden hair, but what registered with me most was that these beings radiated an aura of perfect health and happiness. Immediately I sensed a feeling of goodwill emanating from them which took away any fear I might have had at this sudden meeting. They were wearing grey coveralls and somehow I knew then that they were space beings. I noted with interest that both were bare-headed, with no helmets or other apparatus, and yet they seemed to have no difficulty in breathing Earth air. I have since been asked if there were any physical differences from Earthmen about these space people and I can only say that I saw none -- and why should there be? Are we not all built the same, in the likeness of God?

Then one of them spoke to me in very good English, saying, "Good morning, Arthur Matthews. May we go with you into your workshop?" If this was a surprise, there was a greater one to follow, as he continued; "We are from Venus and we have come to see what you are doing with Tesla's inventions."

Completely taken back, I could only blurt out: "How am I supposed to believe you are from Venus?" The one who appeared to be the leader answered calmly: "When you see our ship, you will believe. But before we go, I will make a sketch of Tesla's Anti-War Machine. No one on Earth but you knows its secret. Will *that* convince you?"

I nodded and led them to my workshop. With a few deft strokes, he drew a sketch for me which I could only accept as the truth. A brief inspection and explanation of the work I was doing on the Tesla devices followed. No comments were made and I was left to assume they were satisfied with my efforts.

Then the two Venusians said they would take me to their spaceship. We walked toward the mountain and soon I was staring wide-eyed at the gigantic proportions of the mother-ship X-12, hardly believing my senses, while my two companions chuckled at my bewilderment. The landed ship, which appeared to be made of grey metal (?), looked like two gargantuan saucers put together rim to rim. Circling these rims about 20 ft. away from the main body of the craft was an unsupported band of material (later referred to as the "Guide Ring") which was not attached to the ship by any visible means and appeared to be held in place by some magnetic force. Penetrating the center of the ship was a tubular shaft 50 ft. in diameter and 300 ft. in height, the top and bottom ends of which protruded from the ringed saucers which were 700 ft. in diameter. The bottom end of this large tube rested on the ground and I could see an opened doorway in which stood two of the crew who greeted us with a hand salute.

My companions invited me in for an inspection tour of the great ship and we stepped into an elevator which I was told had no cables and was operated by will power! We stopped off at the level which was devoted to the storage of some of the 24 small spacecraft this mother-ship carried, ground vehicles and other equipment. The second level comprised the living quarters of the crew, gardens, recreation area, sutdy rooms and a meeting hall. Living quarters were compartments for single persons or "married" couples (for the crew was made up of both sexes) and these units comprised a small hallway, a large living room, bedroom, bathroom with toilet and storage locker. All rooms were carpeted with some form of pliant plastic and the walls were hung with beautiful paintings. I discovered the outer wall of the living room was in fact "see through," giving a full view of space outside. The outer door of each compartment led out on to a small flower-bedded garden. At this point, I commented on the lack of a kitchen in these units and was informed that Venusians never spoil their food by cooking it. They grew their own produce aboard and ate it fresh.

We then came to the recreation area which was covered with some form of simulated grass on which a number of the crew were playing a game somewhat like basketball. This gave me an opportunity to study these Venusians more closely and I noted that they ranged from 5'6" to 6 ft. in height. They were blue-eyed, skin coloring a bronze sun-tan and their hair ranged from golden blonde to a reddish brown. They all appeared in glowing health and their eyes sparkled with a natural *joie de vivre*. Climbing to the third level, I found this was the horticultural section where all their food produce was grown and there were attractive gardens where the crew relaxed and ate their food. The fourth level was divided between storage of more of the small scout ships, heavy material, water supply, etc., and a number of workshops. I had noted that throughout the entire ship all floors were completely covered with some form of plastic material and that all the outer walls were of the same "see through" type. On each wall there was a circular viewing screen, somewhat like television, showing a full view of outer space and the exact position of the X-12 in relation to other planets, and its directional trajectory in space, this changing picture being projected from the control tower to all parts of the ship. I was also informed that built into these walls were "accumulators" for storing solar energy which gave constant light and power to operate heating and air conditioning systems.

We then rose to the exposed top of the tubular shaft which I was told was the control room. My Earthly mind had conjured up visions of all kinds of complex devices to operate this enormous spacecraft, but to my great surprise, there were no visible controls or equipment at all! In the center of the room was a raised circular platform on which had been built a circular couch and seated with their backs to this and facing outward to the North, South, East and West, were four persons - two women and two men. I was informed that these four operators, chosen specially for their great mental powers, controlled and directed this giant ship! It all seemed completely unbelievable until across my doubting mind there flashed the biblical verse: "Faith can move mountains."

My leader-companion then took me to a lower level and introduced me to a lovely woman whom he described as his "life companion." She was indeed a most beautiful creature, with sapphire-blue eyes, golden-blonde hair and her face glowed with an inner spirituality delightful to behold. He stood beside her and said simply: "You may call us Frank and Frances, for we stand for Truth."

I noticed that the girl was seated before a large blank screen and a further wonder was in store for me, as she demonstrated her ability to project onto it thought forms of whatever she was thinking, which appeared on the screen as living motion pictures. To my surprise, she showed me a picture of myself coming out of my house, followed by the scene in my workshop when I spoke with the two space visitors. There followed pictures of Venus, its people, homes and towns and I just stood there over-awed at its natural beauty. And then a strange phenomenon took place which I know will sound as incredible as it did to me at the time, although there is much we do not know about the power of mind over matter. For while I was fully aware that I, Arthur Matthews, was standing in the physical form in a landed spaceship at Lac Beauport, yet at the same time I suddenly became a living part of the projected scenes, mingling with the people of Venus millions of miles away! Here was a great mystery indeed, for I could not only see them but feel them just as if I was truly there in body as well as spirit.

I appeared to be standing at the edge of a vast, cup-like depression. On every side towered tall pillars of basalt, smooth and perfect as if polished by the hand of man. On the farther side of this huge natural theater, a mighty torrent of water descended from the brow of the ebony cliffs in a 1000 foot leap, striking squarely on the edge of the great cup and turning it into a churning mass of foam. Then I saw it was only around the rocky margins of the pool that the water was beaten into foam. The entire center was occupied

by a mass of water perfectly smooth and strangely piled up like a dome of
glass. It was not water such as we know, for streamers of living light of
every imaginable color darted over the shining surface of the great dome, sometimes blending into masses of rose or green or violet and then mingling into a
glittering confusion of rainbow hues.  This whole scene of overwhelming grand-
eur was foiled by a broad band of emerald green turf which framed the central
cup, and dotted here and there were graceful palm trees whose fronds glistened
with diamond drops of spray.

     Then gazing upward, I gasped in surprise for there, poised in the air
above the rim of the waterfall, was a great crystal ball like a gigantic soap
bubble, transparent but gleaming with rainbow hues.  Around its center was a
broad band of gold metal.  This girdle formed the equator and at either pole
was a projecting boss of the same metal from which were suspended, by cables,
inverted cups which hung some distance below the globe.  As it drew nearer, I
saw that the equatorial band was studded at intervals with circular windows of
glass-like material from the center of each projected a long needle which I
assumed was for directing the course of the airship, a theory which later I
found to be correct.  Slowly the great ball sank until the cups touched the
grass and the cables were withdrawn into the metal bosses.  Here, the shining
sphere hung about a foot above the ground, swaying gently.  A moment later, a
circular window swung open and several figures stepped out.

     Then the scene changed and I beheld a rolling, park-like country clustered
with groups of palms and other trees.  In the distance I could discern the wall
of black cliffs and beyond them rose range upon range of snow-capped peaks from
which a wide river wound its way.  In the central plateau about 50 miles in
diameter, the river broadened into a shining lake and then continued its way
until it plunged over the cliffs into the pit of the shining pool.  Returning
my gaze to the immediate scene around me, I realized I was in the center of a
beautiful Venusian town.  Innumerable buildings were spaciously scattered
among groves of trees.  While of varied size, these structures were of the same
general design, consisting of an ellipsoidal roof of prismatic crystal supported on a circular colonnade of marble pillars.  Above them, hundreds of
balloon-like airships darted through the air.  Many of the houses were built
on top of the basalt columns bordering the river and I could see groups of
people standing on the verge of the cliffs.  I then observed, standing on an
elevation, a very large building of the same circular design which I was told
was the community meeting place of these Venusians.

     I then found myself walking with the crew of the X-12, through a broad
avenue of stately palms toward the white pillars of the great assembly hall.
Soon we were climbing a noble stairway flanked by mighty columns until we
stood in the center of a splendid amphitheatre surrounded by tiers of marble
seats in which a large group of people reclined.  As we entered, they all
arose, their hands raised in the Venusian salute and I heard a unanimous cry
of "Brothers!  Goodwill unto you!"  It was then that I realized that these
Venusians wore no garments but stood as nature created them, but such was their
noble build, I could feel no embarrassment, only admiration of their physical
beauty.

     I was led by Frank to a seat at one side of the huge auditorium and he
then addressed me:  "Friend from across space, Earthman Arthur Matthews, we
welcome you.  The people of Venus ask me to speak for them because I can talk
your language freely.  We have brought you here out of no idle curiosity, but
because we believe it lies in our power to offer your world some help in its
present troubled state.  We have a priceless gift to offer you which is known

to us as Truth, but first we would ask you to tell us more of the world in which you live. Tell us something of its history, social conditions, science and what you call religion, and we will then judge if we are right in revealing to you the secret of Truth. Speak in your own tongue, for all will understand your thoughts. Fear only to say that which is not true, for we shall know immediately the true from the false."

Somewhat bewildered, I arose and after a pause, I spoke: "People of Venus: I thank you for your kind welcome and your offer. I do not know what this gift of Truth may be, but if all the radiant health, happiness and beauty I see among you are due to this truth, I greatly desire to know its secret and share it with the people of Earth. But before I tell you something of conditions on my planet, may I first ask a question?"

There were nods of approval and I continued: "Why have you chosen me to speak for Earth instead of going to the leaders of my world? I am a humble person whose name is unknown and I have no power with which to convince few, if any, on Earth."

"We understand your question," Frank replied. "We have chosen you because, as a friend of Tesla, we believe you will tell us the truth. As for your humble origin, did not the Supreme Creator in Whom we of Venus all believe --your God--choose One of lowly birth to spread the truth of your Christian philosophy? In your Bible, you will read "In the Beginning there was the Word" or the Truth as we call it, and of God's desire that His children should believe in the Word. If we decide to pass on this Truth to you, then God will surely see that channels are opened up to you to pass on His Word." In deep humility, I replied: "In the name of Jesus Christ, I thank you."

And then, to the best of my ability, I proceeded to tell the Venusians what I knew of Earth's history. I described the development of war from the days of the cross-bow and sword to its present stage of destructive sophistication. I dealt with what ancient history I knew and briefly brought it up to modern times. I talked on present day social conditions, our technological achievements, a little on medicine, psychology, philosophy, and comparative religion, and then I turned to science. Up to this point, these god-like Venusians had listened to my poor talk with absorbed attention, but as I attempted to explain Earth's concept of physics, there was a great commotion as members of the assembly leaped to their feet and I heard repeated cries clamoring for the Truth! I could only conclude from this that our scientists' present knowledge of physics left much to be desired! A few words from Frank, explaining that I was telling the truth only as I knew it, quieted the group and he apologized to me for the interruption. At the conclusion of my talk, I was invited by Frank and his beautiful companion, Frances, to spend some time with them, and, to my great delight, they took me for a flight in their small airship where I sat back entranced at the glorious landscape unfolding beneath us. And then, as mysteriously as I had been "teleported" to Venus by the thought projection process, I suddenly found myself back in the landed spaceship at Lac Beauport, facing an empty screen.

Over the years of continued landings of the X-12 at Lac Beauport, I was able, by means of Frances' strange ability to project me into her living pictures, to continue my contacts with the Venusians, whom I grew to love for their gentle, courteous ways, their radiant happiness and beauty of mind and body. Always, Frank and Frances acted as my host and hostess and I spent many happy hours with this gracious couple, sometimes wandering on pleasant walks through groves of cinnamon and nutmeg trees, breathing in the soft, perfumed air, sometimes going on fabulous flights of exploration in their airship, and

52

at other times, we relaxed in their beautiful crystal dwelling, discussing many matters, exchanging information on our respective planets, and all the time, I learned more of the harmonious way of life of these happy Venusians. Frank talked freely on all aspects of the life of his people, with one exception -- the nature and meaning of the Truth --- from which I gathered that the time was not yet right for this revelation.

I was amazed at the perfection of the Venusian mode of one planetary government guided by a small council of wise leaders and also at the extreme simplicity of the social relationships of its people who appeared to be one large family bound together by love and understanding. At one time I asked Frank if Frances was his wife. "No, not in the sense your world interprets this word," he replied. "We have mutually elected to become life companions."

"Then surely you have been united by some ceremony such as we call marriage?"

"No, with this mutual desire in our hearts, we have no need for meaningless words."

"So there is nothing to prevent you from separating at any time?"

"Nothing at all."

"Then what we call divorce must be common on Venus," I ventured.

The Venusian couple laughed outright. "As common as the rose voluntarily cuts itself from the bush," remarked Frances with a gentle laugh.

"Let me explain," said Frank. "When Venusian couples unite, because of their knowledge of the Truth, it is impossible for them to make a mistake, for they recognize each other as soul-mates and the union is forever. It is sad that your world lacks this knowledge, for it would appear that such legal ceremonies are necessary because your people are insecure and uncertain of each other."

During one of our aerial excursions over the wooded countryside, I remarked on the absence of any burial grounds and that the word "death" had never been mentioned in our talks. Frank countered with: "How old are you, Arthur?"

"48 years."

"What is the normal life-span on Earth?"

"70 - 100 years."

"Then you will probably be surprised to learn I have seen over 800 summers and Frances over 650."

"You must be joking!" I exclaimed.

"Sickness and old age sap the vitality of the body and within 100 years, it dies." Frank shook his head. "Because we apply the knowledge of the Truth, we know nothing of sickness or old age. True, we finally leave our bodies, not because they are worn out but because our appointed time has come to transfer to another sphere of existence. But a few of us with special missions here, such as those with the required wisdom to govern our planet, may live on in perfect health for thousands of years!" I was left dumfounded at these remarks which seemed more than my Earthly mind could absorb.

And thus the periodic contacts with the Venusians continued, with information exchange and progress reports on my work on the Tesla devices passing between us until finally the great day arrived when Frank informed me that the Venusian Assembly had decided that the gift of Truth should be extended to me and through me, to the people of Earth. You may well imagine my excitement on learning that this great mystery was at last to be revealed to me! It was to take place, Frank said, at the Venusians' most sacred shrine, the "Palace of Truth" and although he spoke of its great beauty, I was little prepared for the further wonders in store for a bewildered Earthling!

First, I was taken to the edge of the cliffs where the river gathered for its final plunge and Frank led the way to a flight of spiralling steps carved out of the solid rock. We descended these steps which eventually entered the rock itself and we came out on to a small platform directly under the mighty waterfall which thundered down to the abyss. With a thrill of horror, I realized we were standing on top of one of the towering basalt columns and I admit I shook with fear. But Frank grasped my hand and led me to a further flight of spiralling steps. Down we went, sometimes passing close to the water whose roar grew louder as we descended, and sometimes passing through tunnels in the rock. Behind us there followed a seemingly endless line of figures. Finally we came to a great cave directly under the fall and the living rock trembled with the force of its tremendous impact. On we went until we passed through an arched opening and stood at last in the Palace of Truth! At the glory of the sight that met my eyes, I let out an involuntary cry of delight and amazement. We stood on a broad shelf of black basalt surrounding a great circular depression about 1000 ft. in diameter which was filled with a mass of colored water which surged and rippled like a sea of rainbows. A closer inspection revealed that it was in fact a floor of living crystal (See Chap. 4, Revelations) and looking up, I saw it was reflecting the underside of the great dome of water in the center of the pool below the waterfall. By some strange magic beyond my comprehension, the crystal lake held this mass of churning, multi-colored water suspended in mid-air, its under-surface reflecting a thousand-fold. It was the most breathtakingly beautiful sight I had ever seen.

While I had been absorbing the indescribably beauty of this natural kaleidoscope, the basalt shelf had been filling with the great company of people assembled for this meeting. Then Frank raised his hand in salute and spoke: "Friend from Earth, the glory you behold is our Palace of Truth and we have brought you here as a fitting place to reveal to you its secret. You have told us truly of the world in which you live and we are grieved at your story. Therefore we hope this revelation in time will lead to a great improvement in conditions on your planet. Make no mistake! We do not worship the Truth. We worship the One God Whom no man may know. As for the Truth, we know not from whence it comes -- only that it fills all space and permeates all things. It is no great mystery confined to our planet alone -- it is free for all to seek and use throughout the universe. You yourself have revealed that you have known the Truth for many years, but you have not recognized it as such. Did not you tell us that your friend, Tesla, had discovered and used the cosmic ray? This, my friend, is the Truth which we also call the Power of Life. It is the essence which animates all living things -- man, animal, vegetable and mineral. It is the vibration which responds to the mind and spirit of all life and once one has learned to use this great natural law wisely, one mind beholds another in all its truth, so that misunderstanding is impossible. Thus it is we are able to understand you when you speak your own language for we see not only the outer shell as you do, but the living mind within that shell. It is because of our understanding of the Truth that we enjoy long life in perfect health, happiness and harmony, that we are able to construct and operate by pure thought our spacecraft and other technological wonders you have seen, erect beautiful dwellings with every comfort and convenience, transmute our planet into beauty and agricultural productivity, effect climate control and avert natural disasters -- in short, we have transformed our planet into a paradise. And all these things, my friend, may be achieved by the people of Earth if they learn to recognize and use the Truth!"

I had listened in some surprise to learn that the Truth should be none other than the cosmic ray, which I knew something about, for Tesla had built his "Scope" and other wonderful inventions to utilize the power of this ray. I knew too, that more than a purely physical force was involved because in harnessing the cosmic ray, Tesla had discovered that it responded to mental vibrations.

But one big question burned in my mind and I asked Frank: "But how can the people of Earth recognize this Truth?"

"We do not see the Truth with the physical eye," he replied. "We see it with an inner eye that lies in the metaphysical area of the mind and which is opened up by spiritual development."

"You seem to forget," I returned, "that most of us on Earth lack this special sixth sense which enables Venusians to visualize mental images produced by the Truth. You can tell a blind man of the light, but you cannot make him see!"

"Arthur, this special faculty is not the exclusive possession of Venusians. It is common to all mankind -- inherent in life itself. For countless generations, your race has lived and died like men who bandage their eyes that they might not see the light! Listen carefully."

And then in words so simple that the humblest person could understand, Frank revealed the secret whereby people of Earth -- if they choose to accept it -- can learn to develop this marvellous sixth sense and the full consciousness of Truth. In essence, it was nothing more or less than to carry out the philosophy of love of God and all His creatures, as taught by Jesus Christ, which in turn, would open up that special spiritual area of the mind to see the Truth!

Then, in ringing tones that sounded like the clear notes of a bugle, Frank addressed me: "Go back to your Earth, Arthur, and tell its people of the things you have seen and the knowledge you have acquired."

"But Frank!" I cried in an anguished voice, "although I shall speak the truth, few will believe me. Most will dismiss my words as, at best, a Utopian fantasy! Many will label me 'crackpot' or worse!"

Frank grasped my shoulders and spoke firmly. "Heed not the words of the foolish. Speak for those with sufficient wisdom to learn. If you only reach a few, your efforts and all the ridicule, will not have been in vain. Go forth with the Word, Arthur -- and God go with you."

With these words still ringing in my ears, I found myself back in full consciousness on the landed X-12. As I prepared to depart, the beautiful woman of countless years rose from her blank screen and with a lovely smile, extended her hand in farewell. Later, from a distance, I watched the great ship rise silently and swiftly and take off into that summer's night of 1961.

# Chapter 2

It was during the fall of 1942 that the X-12 paid me another short visit, Frank wished to talk to me about a very private matter.  DURING THIS VISIT I was lucky to be able to take a good look at the X-12 inside and out, Frank came into my home and after we finished our private talk, we walked down to the landing spot, when we reached the ship, I stood wild eyed looking at that great and wonderful thing, other members of the crew came out, all of them laughing at the surprised look on my face, but what I saw of the outside of that great ship was nothing to the wonders which I was to see and hear, inside.  It was in fact the "Thought-pictures," which first convinced me that this ship and its crew of twenty-four persons, was indeed, as they said, from the planet Venus.  When Frank and I arrived at the ship, he said "Come inside and you may, if you wish, take a good look all over."  I accepted his invitation, and he led me to a door, and we stepped into a small room, which he said was the elevator, in a few seconds, we arrived at the top level, or control room, located at the top of the elevator shaft (about 300 feet high!).  "This is our control room," said Frank.  "You may inspect it."  "But,"I replied, "where are the controls?"  (All I saw in the room was a circular seat, on which sat four persons; two women and two men.  These four took no notice of us, they just sat and looked, so it appeared, directly at the wall).  "These four are our controls," said Frank "But where are the meters," I asked, "and other things which appear to be an important part of our air-craft?  In what manner can you guide, steer and control the power of this large ship without some form of control?"  "Well," said Frank, "perhaps the manner in which we control this ship, that is to say, the means we use, may appear to you earth people an impossibility; every member of our crew is trained in the practical use of 'Thought Power'.  The four members whom you see here, keep the ship under perfect control at all times by the simple application of pure thought.  In order to convince you, or at least try to convince you, that this ship has no other power, you may inspect every inch of it, but I can assure you there is no engine of any kind, either inside or outside.  But, measure carefully, convince yourself.  If you study the question, you will find nothing remarkable about our ability to make a practical use of the power of applied thought.  Every person on earth could, with advantage, do the same.  Millions of you earth people buy the Bible, but how many make a practical use of it?  Christ walked on the water by means of thought power or faith, and did He not say 'The works which I do, you can do, and even greater works than these, because I go to my Father....'?  Do you not see the wonders you earth people could do if you believed in what Christ said?  We of Venus do not consider ourselves any smarter than people of earth, the difference appears to be in the fact that we take it for granted that Christ knew what He was talking about.  We believe in what He said, with the results which you see in our ship, and the way in which we live on Venus."

With those remarks Frank said, "Make a good inspection.  I will wait outside for you, and when you are finished looking for our 'mystery' engine, Francis will continue with her picture show," and left me.  I then had a very careful look around the control room but could find no sign of a motor or material control of any sort.  I then walked down some steps to the 4th level, which was divided between storage of small scout ships, heavy material, water supply, etc. with a number of workshops, but I could find nothing like a power plant. The third level was very much the same, except it had a large horticultural section where all their food was grown, and the lovely gardens where the crew relaxed and ate their food.  A few scout ships were also on this floor.  I had a good look all over and then continued going down to the second level, so far no sign of a power plant.  I found the second level the same as the others, except a part comprised the living quarters of the crew.  It had flower gardens, a recreation area, study rooms and a meeting hall.  Living quarters were compartments for single persons or married couples; each unit comprised of a small hallway, a large living room, bedroom, bathroom with a flush toilet and storage locker.  But still no sign of a power plant or any material controls.  After a good look, I walked down to the first level which was devoted to the storage of some more small space craft and ground vehicles, work shops and other equipment.

"Well," I thought, "if there is any motor on this ship it must be made of invisible and sizeless material!" for there was not an inch of space anywhere on that ship which I had not inspected.  To be sure, I would have to take a good look on the outside of the ship.  During my inspection trip, I noted with delight the beautiful floor covering, of many colours, which appeared to be made of a synthetic material, very soft to walk on.  The walls were hung with beautiful paintings, none of which were of the 'modern' kind, and each living room had a see through window giving a full view of the outside.  During my visit a number of the crew were playing a game somewhat like basketball.  This gave me an opportunity to study these people more closely and I noted that they were exactly the same as earth people - at least I could see no difference.  They were from about 5'6" to 6' in height, some were blue-eyed, others appeared to have green and brown eyes.  Skin colouring appeared a bronze sun-tan and their hair in many shades from golden blond to a reddish brown.  They all appeared in glowing health and their eyes sparkled with that health.  After my careful inspection of the inside of this great ship, I walked outside where Frank and Frances were waiting for me.  Having partly recovered from my surprise on seeing the ship, I now took a more careful look at its outside.  It was indeed a strange looking object.  I found it hard to believe my senses, and still thought I must be dreaming, my feelings were no doubt reflected on my face, because my two companions gave amused chuckles at my bewilderment.  The landed ship which appeared to be made of grey coloured metal looked like a big egg, and circling it, about twenty-feet away from the main body of the ship, was an unsupported ring of the same grey coloured material.  I found out later that it was a "guide-ring" (whatever that meant?).  This guide ring, which was over seven-hundred feet in diameter, was not attached to the main body of the ship by any visible means.  I thought, "Maybe the power plant is inside this ring?"  In the center of the ship was the control tower, and elevator, with a door at the lower end, which at the moment rested on the ground.  This tower is 300 feet in height, with 50 feet protruding from the main body at each end, that is 50 feet protruding from the main body at each end (50 feet at the top and 50 feet at the bottom) which made the main body 200 feet high and 700 feet in diameter.  After a careful inspection, I could find no sign of a motor, unless it was inside that guide ring.  It was 20 feet in diameter and depending on what kind of motor, it was large enough to hold it.  I said as much to Frank.  "Well," he answered, "all right my fine doubter, you may now go inside that guide ring."  I said nothing, but at the moment I failed to see how I could go inside.  It turned out to be easy.  Frank led me back inside the ship, up to the third level, then to a door which he opened, and I could see the guide ring about twenty feet away.  I then noted a door in its side.  Frank pushed a botton which was on the wall near the door.  In a few seconds, the door in the guide ring opened and a platform came out of the door opening towards us.  In a few more seconds Frank had the platform attached and I noticed the platform had hand-holds for which I was very glad - for we were about 150 feet from the ground/  Frank said "Come with me," and walked across the platform and into the guide ring, as I followed close behind.  "Go all around," said Frank, "make a good inspection.  You may go alone, I will wait here for you.  Take your time."

Without further words I started my walk around the inside of this mystery ring, and what a mystery it turned out to be!  I do not know where the light came from, there were no windows, but I could see clearly, and the mystery proved to be - nothing!  A completely empty tube!  How did it work?  How did it 'guide'?  How was it supported?  Questions, questions: no answers.  I could not find any power plant, just empty nothing.  I walked completely around inside that tube to find Frank waiting for me.  "Well my good friend," he asked, "did you find what you were looking for?"  "No Frank," I replied, I found nothing.  Will you tell me the answer to this mystery?"  "Yes," said Frank, "I will tell you but its a big secret.  You must not tell any one, do you agree?"  "Yes," I said, "I agree."  "Well," said Frank, "I have told you but you doubt.  This great mystery is no more or less than the power of thought.  You have made a most careful inspection: you found only empty space, did you not?"  "Yes," I replied, "I did inspect your great ship, outside and in, and also the ring, to the best of my ability.  I found no sign of any power plant.  Therefore, at least for the moment, I must believe all you say.  I believe in the power of thought but I must admit, my earth-man faith is not very strong."

# Chapter 3

The third visit of the great Space-Ship X-12 was a few days after Tesla died. Members of the crew had attended the funeral with over a thousand people, some of whom had come from far off corners of the earth to pay their last respects to the inventor of the 20th century.

Frank said that he and Frances had been with Tesla a few days before he died, and that he had died a happy man. "And," said Frank with a smile, as he handed me a large envelope, "he told me to be sure to give you this. It contains some very important papers concerning the work which you must now continue alone." When Frank and I finished our talk about my work of the future, Frances said she had something to say. "Yes," said Frank, "Frances will give us a little lecture which could be a greater help to your world than all the inventions of man." Frances smiled, "I haven't very much to say but I am sure you will like this message which your old friend wrote only a few short days before he left this earth."

Frances then read this message, the last words of this great man who did so much for mankind:

"One of the most important facts in life, even if we do not always see it, is that we live only one day! The human struggle is mostly for one day, we can not live to-morrow before it comes. If we can live consistently for one day, we may hope to do the same the next, and the next, and so on to th eend. A day has a rounded completeness; it is a little world of life. 'One day is like to all days,' wrote Montaigne. 'He who has lived a day has lived an age,' said La Bruyere. 'Every day is a little life,' said another; 'those therefore that dare lose a day are dangerously prodigal; those that mis-spend it desperate.' As our habits, thoughts, words, and actions are on one day, of that same character they will most likely partake as day is added to day and goes on to make up the months and years. If we can get through one day without giving way to temptation, then come night and sleep, and to-morrow we start afresh for another period of hours in which to be strong and true. On this day then, we are each of us bound to begin by asking ourselves, 'Is my conscience void of offense both before God and man?' 'Do I condemn myself in anything which I allow?' When I have been saying that as one day of our lives is, so will in all probability the rest be, I am only insisting on the blessing of being able to take each unit of our lives as it comes, and making the best of it, making it perfect, making it ideal. One day well spent is a pledge for those that are coming. Abraham Lincoln said, 'The struggle of to-day is not altogether for to-morrow; it is for the vast future also.' Every day is a gift I receive from heaven; let me enjoy to-day that which it bestows upon me; and to-morrow belongs to no one."

End of Tesla's last words. May this message bring joy to every heart who reads it.

Health is a mental condition, physical well being depends on one's mental condition. All bad habits, such as smoking, strong drink, drugs, etc. depend on a mental factor: a sick mind breeds a sick body. Bad habits indicate a sick mind and a sick physical condition, and when the majority of people suffer from bad habits the end result is a sick world; so said Tesla. And while we are on the subject of a sick world I would like to quote from a little booklet by Perry F. Rockwood who has granted permit to copy. Mr. Rockwood has the same idea as Tesla and Frank, the people of earth are wasting their time on rubbish and there is no time to waste. I quote in part -

"The greatest peril to western civilization today is not from communism, but from the constant erosion of faith in God. Large numbers of supposedly religious people simply do not believe in God. The curse of our day that has brought about this faithless way of living is so-called evolution. Our young people are being taught by unscientific text-books about the biggest fraud ever brought into the class-rooms. And our young people, in order to be sophisticat-ed, allow themselves to be brain-washed into thinking that there is no personal God who created this universe. This message is offered to those who are wil-ling to think independently of archaic teaching that characterizes so many class-rooms today. Those who criticize the Bible the most read it the least, and know little or nothing about it.

"WHAT is Science? Can we improve upon the Dictionary's answer? 'Know-ledge gained and verified by exact observation and correct thinking; especially as methodically formulated and arranged in a rational system.' This defini-tion takes you out of the realm of speculation. It disposes of such terms as 'theory' and 'hypothesis,' making them possible servants of Science, but never its synonyms. Science is the 'verification of knowledge by exact observation and correct thinking' and is the highest accomplishment of which the human mind is capable. Not every man, however, who cries 'Eureka' has found it. What is the Bible? The Bible is the 'God-breathed' Book, written by holy men of God who spake as they were moved by the Holy Ghost------. The remarkable evidence of the skepticism of this generation is that so many educated leaders and preachers are willing to throw away the fact of the Verbal Inspiration of the Bible. At the same time they try to tell us that God stimulated the thought of the Bible but did not determine the speech; that some parts of the Bible are literally true, and others only allegory or myth; that some are factual, others are fiction; that some are to be treated with credence, and others with criti-cism; that all must come to the test of one's inner consciousness or the logi-cal processes of man's wisdom and, at that court, be either accepted or rejected. The Bible itself is God's special revelation to man and this revelation is truth absolutely. The pursuit of scientific research, on the other hand, can never achieve more than relative truth. The growth of science is a history of constantly increasing knowledge resulting from human investigation or discovery. The Bible, on the other hand, bears eternal, absolute truth. The pages of scientific research are replete with examples of abandoned ideas, discarded theories, and repealed laws resulting from a continuous process of adapting earlier ideas to more recently discovered scientific data. The Bible is God's revelation and does not change with the changes of men. Evolution is a theory of a materialistic philosophy of life based upon suppositions which have not been verified by science. Evolution is the foundation stone of communism, based upon the false theory of automatic and inevitable progress. It is the founda-tion stone of militarism based upon the concept of the survival of the fittest. Two world wars were the logical outcome of evolutionary teaching and we are now preparing for the next world war. Evolution is also the foundation stone of atheism based upon a materialistic concept of life. The word 'evolution' is often abused. The casual speaker talks of the 'evolution' of the telephone, the 'evolution' of the electric light, and other products of man's industry and intelligence. The proper word here is 'development.' All of these mechanical improvements came about because of direct supervision and control. Organic evolution in its simplest definition can be best expressed by the word trans-mutation. The theory admits of no active intelligence in control, and design is foreign to the entire process. Evolution is not scientifically possible. First, 'Acquired-characters' are not transmitted to or inherited by the offspring

60

as the evolutionists declare. The habit of foot binding, for example, common among Chinese women for centuries has not led to any inherited deformity of the foot. Our domestic chicken is a descendant of the Roman fowl and no essential change has taken place in 2000 generations of breeding." End of quote from the booklet by Perry F. Rockwood.

If any one would sincerely like to know if they are standing on a sure foundation, I suggest they write for the booklet, for if you have been misled to believe in evolution, you are heading some place fast, but you can be sure it is not Heaven! or a "higher" level. It is your life, and you are free to do as you like with it. But, whatever you do, don't try to mix evolution with Divine Love. We either believe without question in the Bible, or we do not believe. To take a half-way stand is a luke-warm attitude and if you wish to know what that means, read Revelation, Chapter 3.

# Chapter 4

As I watched from a distance, the great X-12 rise silently and swiftly, and take off into the sky, I wondered exactly what the present day scientific knowledge concerning the "Cosmic Rays" amounted to. When Tesla first discovered them, way back in 1893, the scientific world laughed at him. They said no such rays existed! Tesla proved they did, that much is history. So today, due to the attitude of supposed scientific experts - who in reality are not truly scientific, for the truly scientific mind never doubts - very little is known about the subject, but some wise men have discovered that our atmosphere is continually being bombarded by atomic particles from outer space. These are known as "primary cosmic rays." These high speed particles are mostly said (by the above named 'experts') to be protons, and they say that when these 'protons' go crashing through our atmosphere, they break up some of Earth's atoms, the particles of which are (so they say) called "secondary cosmic rays" - which statement, coming from doubters who said cosmic rays did not exist, is something to think about! They also say that both of these minute cosmic rays are extremely energetic and can enter and pass through almost any form of matter. Every minute thousands of them pass through everything on earth, including man. Our scientists admit that they do not know exactly where the primary cosmic rays come from. In my opinion the reason for their lack of knowledge is because they neglect to study the Bible! For in it is the place where Tesla first discovered them, 35 years before the scientific world "experts" thought maybe they might exist.

The Great Nebula in Orion appears to the naked eye as only a single hazy star. But when viewed through a large telescope this great mystery of the heavens is revealed to be a tremendous cavern, perhaps nineteen trillion miles across. Our entire solar system would be lost therein - could not the cosmic rays come from there?

After the great space ship left, I received many messages from its crew, but they did not return after that last visit in 1961, until 1969. It was during the evening of January 21st, 1969 that a number of friends came to visit me, and if possible, listen to a message on the "Tesla-Scope." No sound was heard from it until around 10 p.m. after we had been talking for three hours; when the voice of Frank was heard very clearly, with the same old message which I had received on the Scope, and recorded so many times since that first visit of the great X-12 in the spring of 1941. I will repeat this message for the benefit of those who may not have heard it (apart from the omission of certain personal messages connected mainly with my continued work for Tesla). The following is the message which I first received in 1941, and which, in essence, has been repeated over the years; in fact it is the message which we can read in the Bible. However, this message which I have personally heard by means of the Tesla-Scope, from 1941 right up to recent months (1969) comes from real live persons, who say they are aboard a space craft, which they call the "X-12" - a mother ship. Here then, is the message: - "When you first receive this message, you will, like most earth people, doubt. This is one of the strange things we find about the people of Earth, their continued doubting. They say they believe in God, but they doubt! They say God can cure their sickness and their troubles, but they doubt. Therefore, we expect you to doubt also. You will wonder if we really come from the planet Venus, do we come from outer space? And you will wonder how we are able to talk to you in your own language. We use English at this time because you, our friend Matthews, understand that language, but we have made a study of every language used by mankind. Actually, we would prefer to transmit our thoughts by the use of mental waves. As we look down on Earth, we note the greatest confusion and misunderstanding. Instead of acknowledging the One God and looking towards Him for enlightenment, we find you all over the earth running hopelessly and helplessly in pursuit of many things you think will increase your personal happiness, and yet you wonder why you continue to suffer. We hear you, year after year, asking the same question, 'Why must we suffer?' 'Why do we still have wars, sickness, poverty, famine and death?' 'Why does pure joy always run away faster than we can so that we can never catch up with it?' The answers to these questions are to be found in the fact that instead of turning upwards to God, your thoughts are earthbound and you judge only by what you see in others around you, the vast majority of whom are sick, unhappy and full of bad habits, doubting the existence of the Supreme Being, and futilely, you follow the crowd. Your earth is full of hate and misery, and this condition has come to be accepted as the rule for mankind on earth. This is not how God intended life to be on your beautiful planet, but very few of you obey the law of God. Many of you attend some form of religious service on your Sundays, but how many earth people carry out God's law in their everyday lives? We are amazed and saddened to find how much of your lives is devoted to inventing and using destructive machines with which you murder each other. We see you spending vast sums of money pretending to bring peace on earth, when you should know that the only way of obtaining peace is free - through Christ: Love. There is no other way, so why waste your time and money?

"We ask this question realizing that most earth people have known for almost 2,000 years, that the only way to secure peace on earth and goodwill towards your fellow men, is by following the teachings of Jesus Christ whom a God of love sent to your planet to bring spiritual enlightenment to mankind.

"Therefore we can only sadly conclude tha t the people of earth must be suffering from some form of mental sickness which can only BE CURED BY THE ADOPTION OF CHRIST'S PHILOSOPHY OF LOVE. You have heard all this before and much of what we say may fall on deaf ears, but our thoughts are directed to those few of the earth people who have sufficient mental and common sense power to think clearly and to know right from wrong. These few have been placed among you to help others to live as God intended you to live, to think clearly and to know right from wrong, and to grow in a manner to be of service to the great, all-knowing, all-loving God, and to all His creatures. Your present behaviour is the reason for the continued visits to earth by those of the space people. It is our duty to warn you, remind you, that if you continue to refuse to obey the law of God, you will surely destroy yourselves, and we shall not have many people to pick up when the earth is about to be destroyed. To help the people on earth, we brought down one of our own to live among you. During a trip to earth a child was born on our space ship which we call "The X-12." We landed our ship at midnight, on July 9, 1856 and we decided to leave this boy on your earth. This boy was Nikola Tesla, we left him on your earth in the hope that his higher mental power would enable him to help your world, which even then was torn by hate and war, to come out of the darkness into the light. During the years between 1856 and 1943, we landed many times on earth, but we found no improvement there. At the death of Tesla in 1943, we landed again and attended his funeral. We were saddened to find that the earth people had used the gifts of Tesla and other great inventors only to satisfy their greed and lust for power, that the same evil conditions existed on earth and that its people continued to expend their energy on war and killing their own kind, which is contrary to God's law which clearly states, "Thou shalt not kill." These things are beyond our understanding, for Venus in all its history, has

63

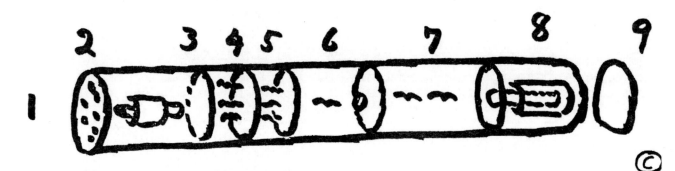

THE TESLA SCOPE FOR SPACE COMMUNICATION. BY  ARTHUR  MATTHEWS

CONCEIVED BY NIKOLA TESLA IN 1898. to communicate with planet VENUS.

First model built  1918, Second model built by Arthur Matthews

with Tesla  1938.  Re-Built the 1938 model in  1947.

Third completly new design model  built by Arthur Matthews  1967.

Adapting the microminiature parts, Thus reducing size to six feet

long and four inches in diameter. see sketch of the 1967 model.

--------oooo---------
"Q"GLASS VACUUM TUBE ENCLOSED IN WOODEN BOX 9ft long,5 in diameter.
LEGEND

1-AUDIO OUTPUT

2_PICK _UP

3-CONVERTER

4-AUTOMATIC CONTROL CHAMBER.

5-GAS CHAMBER.

6-CONVERTER.

7-RECEIVED ENERGY CONTROL.

8-DARK ROOM.

9-HEAD(Q_GLASS FILTER).

TESLA SCOPE   1967 - 6 ft long,    4 in diameter

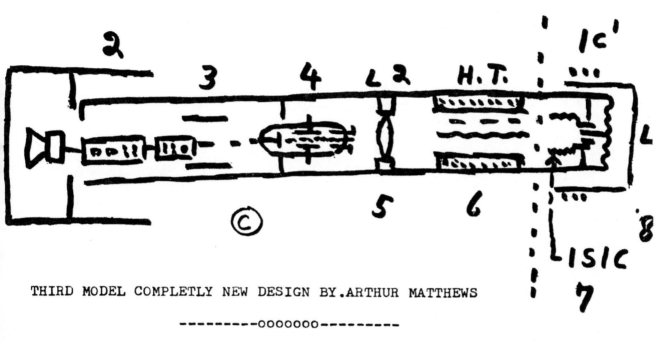

THIRD MODEL COMPLETLY NEW DESIGN BY.ARTHUR MATTHEWS

---------oooooooo---------

LEGARD

1-AUDIO OUTPUT.

2-AMPLIFYER.

3-CONVERTER.

4-FILTER GAS CHAMBER.

5-FILTER.

6-RECEIVED ENERGY CONTROL

7-AUTOMATIC CONTROL CHAMBER.

8-HEAD.   Q"   GLASS FILTER.

never had war. We have but one purpose in life; to serve God, and this we do with all our energy of body and mind, and because we do this, our mental power grows stronger with age. We remain in perfect health until the day we die. We enjoy perfect harmony, health and happiness with our loved ones all the days of our lives. We have no place in our hearts for selfish desires because we know and believe that God's law is good and therefore we have no need of man-made laws. Lack of faith in God has left your earth in the Dark Ages and you will never progress or know peace of mind, true happiness and complete harmony until you learn to renew your faith and to become higher in your thinking and living than the crawling things, which you now appear to copy. To overcome hatred, and prevent wars, you must learn to remove every trace of national pride and racial discrimination, for there is, in fact, only one race of mankind whom God created. The truth of God's Law may be learned by all people on earth. You have a book, probably the most important book in your history, called the Bible, which contains the truth for all those with eyes to see. It teaches the only way in which mankind should live, for the law of God is Love.

"We suggest that you turn to the teaching of Christ for the only solution to all of earth's problems. At present, the law of earth men appears to be mainly one of hate, they are always fighting and killing each other, war is murder. We of Venus do not understand how you can truly call yourselves 'Christians' for Christ taught only love. If you continue to make war, you will bring about the destruction of your planet, and in this regard we refer you to the book of Isaiah. We have tried to talk to the people of earth for many hundreds of years, but without good results. Some of our people landed on earth thousands of years ago, as you may read in your Bible which contains many references to the visits of space people to earth.

"We bring this same message to you in the hope that whoever receives it, will extend it word for word, to as many epople on earth as possible. You cannot receive our message on your regular radio systems, but we hope that others will give due honour to Tesla, and succeed in building his Scope, by means of which we can pass on our vital message in the dark days ahead. We cannot interfere with your destiny which by God-given free will you have created for yourselves. We can only hope that some of you will listen to Christ, asking God for wisdom. We have repeated this message for so many hundreds of years, can we ever hope to see the people of earth learn and live by it?

"You should. It is your only hope, your only salvation."

End of message.

Chapter 5

A very loud buzzing almost drowned out the last words of Frank's message
and when Frances tried to talk a few moments later, it was impossible to understand a word, the loud buzzing completely covered the beautiful voice of our
good friend. I managed to hear that she wished to give me 12 meditations on
the good life, and though the strange static prevented her doing so at that
time, I knew that my Venusian friends would make further attempts to communicate this message of importance. They tried repeatedly, but each time Frances
words of wisdom were drowned by the crackling sound of a loud static, until
one night, I managed to receive a few words from Frank and I understood him to
say, "Expect us on April 15." Can you imagine my excitement on hearing those
words? I had heard from them via the Tesla-Scope, but they had not landed on
my place since 1961. Now I was to enjoy a visit within a few weeks, but as
usual, I must not tell anyone, not even my dearest friend, for walls have
ears. I had listened with mounting excitement to Frances' and Frank's words,
for they both repeated the message to make sure that I heard correctly. It
was thrilling indeed to learn that the great X-12 would visit me again after
an absence of 8 years, and I wondered deeply at the portent of the special
messages that made such a personal visit necessary. In the few weeks that
followed, I waited with growing impatience for the arrival of the X-12. As I
had received no indication of the exact time that the space ship would arrive,
I had set up the Tesla-Scope to receive warning of the approach of the X-12
during the period from April 10 to 15. I kept constantly alert for the alarm
signal and must confess I had very little sleep. When April 14 arrived, with
still no warning of the approach of the X-12, I decided to keep vigil day and
night. Shortly after midnight I went outside to check on weather conditions.
It was a dry, fine night, but with low-hanging clouds, ideal for a concealed
landing of the large spaceship. Back in the house I waited it out. It was
around 1:30 A.M. when the alarm signal on the Tesla-Scope rang shrilly and
although I was expecting it, I was startled almost out of my shoes. I ran to
the door for I wanted to see the great ship land, but as I fumbled with the
door latch, it got ahead of me. Noiselessly like a silent cloud, the X-12 had
landed in the large hollow of my big meadow, and as I ran towards it, there it
stood in all its silver-gray glory, and once again I marvelled at its gigantic
proportions. Then a door in the base of the spaceship slid open and framed
against a background of light stood the figures of my two Venusian friends,
Frank and Frances, a wonderful welcoming smile on their faces. They were wearing their usual space coveralls, made of some loose, pliant material quite unknown to me, but fastened tightly at the wrists and ankles and with a wide
flat belt around the waist. Both were bare-headed, but even in the half light
I could see the gleam of their golden-blonde hair, Frank's cut short and Frances'
falling in soft waves to her shoulders. They made a handsome, well built
couple, Frank standing about 6 feet in height and his beautiful companion about
5 ft. 8 inches. They came forward to meet me with a warm embrace as we ex-
changed mutual greetings. Then Frank said: "Come, let us go into your house.
We wish to talk to you." Frank's first message to me was a purely personal
one. There was a grave problem in my life regarding the health and well-being
of a dear friend, which had been causing me deep concern. To my great surprise,
my space friends knew every detail of my problem and were quick in extending
sympathetic understanding and helpful advice, which brought great comfort. He
then discussed with me some special plans for building a new workshop further
north, near Forestville, Quebec, in which I was to carry out further scientific
work on the Tesla ideas. Then Frances stepped forward, a beautiful smile on

her lovely face. "And now, Arthur," she said, "I will give you, without the interference experienced on the Tesla-Scope, my Meditations on the Good Life, a gift to the people of Earth, with love and prayer for you all, in my heart." She paused, as we settled comfortably in my living room to listen to her words, then with a silvery ripple of soft laughter she commenced.

"My first message is of such simplicity that many of you will no doubt laugh, but this is exactly what I want you to do, for my words concern the great value of a smile in all human relationships. In short, I want to talk to you tonight about Pleasantness of Disposition. My friends, you must never under-rate the inestimable power for good in a pleasant manner towards all creatures, circumstances and life in general. A charming smile, a pleasant word or two, will instantly dispel the anger or hard feelings of those ill-disposed towards you, for a genuine smile is a positive radiation of light in which the shadow of negativity cannot exist. We cannot emphasize strongly enough the vital importance of a pleasant disposition, for it is the Golden Key to a happy, healthy life. Did you know that if you cultivate a pleasant disposition, if you smile and laugh a lot, your physical body cannot be assailed by many diseases which are caused by purely mental depression and unnatural anxiety? This is the Divine Law, my friend, and if you desire the two greatest blessings of life, Health and Happiness, they can be yours by means of the Christ-Rule, which is the simple act of being pleasant both to yourself and to all others. It is even the secret of acquiring peace on your earth. Does not your Bible speak of "Peace on earth and goodwill towards men of good will?" This, of course, is nothing new to you. You have been told about it many times, in many ways, by many people. Why is it then that the people of earth cannot learn so simple a lesson with such happy results? As we look down upon you, we see so many of you going about your daily lives with grim expressions on your faces. Some of you will immediately say that life on earth is grim, but dear ones, can't you realize that you are only adding to its grimness by this negative attitude? If you want brighter conditions on earth, all of you have it in your power to bring about this happier state of affairs by development of a cheerful outlook. A pleasant manner and a glowing smile; it is so simple as that. Surely you know that a smile is the most contagious thing on earth; give one and it will be multiplied many times. Some of you may ask, what exactly is Pleasantness? It is a precious jewel indeed, for Pleasantness is a many-faceted diamond, with many forms of expression. In essence, it is the simple act of extending goodwill to yourself and to others and particularly those who may hate you, for you see, it is also a form of self protection because the light you thus emanate cannot be penetrated by the forces of darkness. A pleasant personality entails an optimistic outlook on life, always looking for the Good and Beautiful which exists everywhere as your Bible says; "Seek, and ye shall find." Pleasant ness should be reflected in your every thought, word and deed. It will add an IRRESISTABLE CHARM TO YOUR PERSONALITY BRINGING INNER JOY TO YOURSELF and happiness to others. Since Pleasantness is such an attractive quality, why is it that Earth people in general, do not include it among the avowedly important elements of character building? We watch, with great admiration, many of you teaching your children to be honest, truthful and unselfish, but is not pleasantness the highest form of unselfishness? Of course it is, for it is a positive outpouring of goodwill which brings joy to others and immediately puts them at ease, and furthermore, it brings the reciprocal reward of returned pleasantness. In short, it makes everyone happy. How then can the people of Earth, weighed down by fears and anxieties, develop this gracious art of Pleasantness? Well, to break the acquired habits of many years, brought about by the incomplete understanding of the true meaning of life, is not I realize an easy task. So may I, with love in my heart, suggest a few steps to develop a pleasant personality and urge those of you who are parents or teachers to pass on this invaluable knowledge to your little children.

(1) Practice the art of smiling sincerely, not pretending, at work, at play and particularly in your contacts with others. Be generous with your smiles. They cost you nothing but a slight movement of your facial muscles, and you will be amazed at what you receive in return.

(2) When you talk to others, smile at them and make pleasant remarks. Never miss an opportunity to pass on a genuine compliment. This is valuable therapeutic psychology, for it not only gives pleasure but encourages the recipient to live up to the compliment.

(3) To be easy to get on with is the description of a notable characteristic. To please, it is not necessary to have youth or beauty, or even manners. Charm is something in voice or expression which makes you feel better disposed to your race to look at or listen to. We need not care whether pleasant people are highly educated, they do something far greater; they practically demonstrate the great theorem of the livableness of life.

(4) How many well meaning folk need warning, to not let their good be evil spoken of and your principles discredited because the religion you profess seems, in your practice of it, unlivable, unlovable. You wish people to read something-of faithful character in your example; take care that they do not take you for a hypocrite.

(5) To induce an admiring love for what is good by your conduct, is an aim you will never reach if you are unpleasant, ungracious, unkind. Remember what Christ said, "Judge not, forgive men, give to him that asketh of thee, blessed are the peacemakers, do good to them that hate you."

"And now, Arthur, our dear friend, let me read a little verse which we of Venus learn. --------

'Although it takes so many months,
To make a single year,
Yet far more quickly than you think,
The months will disappear;
The very centuries have wings,
New years grow old and grey;
The work which you intend to do,
Begin it, friend, to-day.
So many months, so many weeks,
But soon they will be passed;
There is but one short life to live,
Each year may be the last.
To yesterday there is no door,
To-morrow may not be.
Today is yours, but nothing more
Belongs to you or me.
Within a single fleeting hour,
How many minutes lie?
But even as you wait to count,
Will sixty moments fly.
If you've a tender word to say,
A kindly deed to do,
Suppose you do it just this day?
I would, if I were you! ' "

With those charming words Frances ended her meditations and we walked outside. As we walked towards the X-12 Frank remarked "We must leave you now Arthur, while it is still cloudy, but do not be sorry; we will come again, and soon. In the meantime let us assure you, you will receive good news. Continue the good work, prove your faith, worry is lack of faith, so do not worry."

"Thanks for the good advice," I said, "I will do my best but there are many questions which I would like you to answer. Time goes fast, who would believe it is almost eight years since you were last here. Have you time to answer one question?" Frank smiled and nodded, "We will stay a short time," he said, "but I must warn you that if the sky brightens, we will have to take off immediately. But speak on, I will try to answer your question." "Well, Frank," I asked, "can you tell me something about this thing which we on earth call 'Gravity'? Can we ever hope to free ourselves from it?" Frank's deep blue eyes scanned mine searchingly. "An intriguing question," he replied. "One thing I know, and which I am sure you know also, is the fact (and all else is only theory) that Gravity is a name used for the unknown force that draws all things towards a center of attraction. It is a Divine Law, and as with all Divine Law - it is forever. But what exactly do you mean by 'freedom from gravity'? Do you mean no gravity at all - or an easy means of lifting yourselves from earth? We of Venus have that power by means of applied "thought" or 'faith.' But we do not remove or interfere, or try to interfere, with the natural force of gravity. Let me explain a little more about gravity. Nothing new in what I can tell you, I think you have as much information about the subject as we have, but as you ask me, I will tell you all that we of Venus know. Gravity consists of two distinct parts, centrifugal force due to a planet's rotation, plus the force of natural attraction of the planet. If the attractive force of planet earth could be stopped, or counteracted, and the centrifugal force remained, all loose material on earth, including air, water andmost buildings, would leave earth forever and fly off into space. If the centrifugal force should also be stopped or counteracted and gravity made equivalent to zero, physical bodies would have no weight. The pressure that the upper strata of earth's atmosphere exerts on the lower strata would cease to exist, the gaseous air would expand and leave the earth, followed by the water which would vaporize. The moon, held in its orbit by the attraction of the earth, would leave it and many other drastic changes would occur.

"If conditions changed so that the human body was no longer subject to gravity, the change would prove fatal, for your physiological and psychological processes would be so deranged you would quickly die under the new conditions. Such conditions imply that the air, water and food which enter the body changed from a condition in which they had weight to one in which they did not.

"Much more could be said, but it would all amount to the same thing. Gravity is one of God's natural laws. It is an exact law and therefore perfect, and if man could upset it, he could not exist. Man cannot improve God's law, but we can make use of them. I believe 'thought' to be the greatest power in existence, and it is by the use of this power that we can overcome the force of gravity. Earth man could learn to use this power, by the practice of perfect faith (not blind faith) by the irrefutable belief that it can be done.

"God be with you, our friend, and with us always, as we work together for spiritual progress and peace on earth."

With the ending of those words Frank and Frances stepped into the X-12. The door closed behind them, seconds later the great spacecraft rose silently and was soon lost behind the clouds, leaving me with many questions in my mind and wondering when they would return.............

## Chapter 6

In early August, 1969, I started off by car for a trip out to Western Canada. Everything went well until I came near to Sault Ste Marie, Ontario. There I met with an accident on the road. This occurred on a gravelly stretch of new construction, when without any warning and in a restricted speed zone, a car shot by at a very high speed, sending up a shower of stones which smashed my car window, sending a piece of broken glass into my left eye, and a slight cut on my left hand, so that I could not continue. I tried to have repairs made at a number of service stations, but they all had the same excuse, no glass on hand to fit, and it would require at least four days to obtain some.

I decided to return to Quebec City, so I patched up the window with clear plastic and headed home via highways 17 and 69, then on 401. Lucky we had no rain, so I took my time stopping at Brockville, Ontario, for two nights and during the time I was there, I received a message from a friend who was posted at the Army Camp at Gagetown, N. B. He said that a large Space Ship had been seen by hundreds of army personnel and he wanted me to go there just as soon as possible. I left Brockville at 4 A.M. and arrived at Quebec City around noon, where a service station applied a new window to my car, which required a little more than one hour. I then drove home to Lake Beauport which is about 16 miles from the station where they fixed the window; by the time I fixed up a light lunch and had a wash, it was almost 3 P.M. I then headed for up-town Quebec City, over the old Quebec Bridge, and then along the No. 2 highway, east; Gagetown here we come! But it was much too far to reach that night. I arrived at Notre-Dame du Lac around 8 P.M. where I stayed for the night. I left after breakfast at 6 A.M. and arrived at Gatetown at 11, and as it was a nice day, I enjoyed a picnic lunch before looking for my friend, whom I located around 12:30. We then went to the place where the Space Ship was seen and I made a very careful inspection, using the special detectors designed by Tesla. I also extended my investigation by questioning the local residents and Army personnel who say they saw the large space craft land. All their descriptions tallied perfectly with that of the X-12. On my return home a few days later, I set up the Tesla Scope, which I had dismantled for my expected long trip out west.

It was towards the end of August, 1969, that I received a message from Frank via the Tesla Scope. It was a request, and it concerned a very earth-bound matter. During their visit to me on April 15, 1969, while in my house, Frank had read a news item which appeared in a U.F.O. paper which was published in Vancouver, B.C. The story concerned a large piece of metal, which was said to have been picked up near Quebec City in 1960. The person who wrote the story said it was a mystery because no one had been able to find out exactly what it was, and the writer went on to say that members of a Canadian science club thought that it might have fallen from space. They said it weighed about 3,000 pounds.

Frank was interested because of the statement he read, which said the metal might be of extra-terrestrial origin, and as this could be interesting, he wanted me to make some tests on it with him. Frank then gave me instructions on how to make the tests, using a Tesla 'Bridge' and a tape recorder. The piece of metal was at Ottawa, Ontario, where as per the instructions which I received from Frank, I made a very careful test. In fact I made three complete tests, with a number of persons present, by means of the Tesla Bridge. I was able to transmit the information recorded over the Tesla Scope directly to Frank, who then made a careful analysis, and according to his findings, it compared exactly with some other pieces of iron which were a part of the first Quebec Bridge which fell in 1906!

When I asked Frank if he could give me an idea of the actual composition and percentage of the various metals found in the chunk, he said that knowing the actual percentage of the various metals would prove nothing, and would be a waste of his time, for our test proved beyond any doubt that it had never been in space. It is exactly the same composition as other blocks found in the same location.

## Chapter 7

Christmas Eve, 1969. I had just arrived from Montreal where by the grace of God my problem had been solved. as promised by our two Venusian friends, Frank and Frances. I had driven from Val Morin, which is 45 miles north of Montreal, a very good road in fine weather, but I had a blinding snow-storm for most of the 45 miles, with slow orders all the way. Lucky for me the balance of the 212 mile journey was fine and clear all the way to Quebec. I was a bit tired when I arrived home, and decided to rest before unloading my car, but no sooner lay down to rest when the alarm on the Tesla-Scope sounded. "Of all things," I thought, "a Christmas message?" It was the voice of Frank. "We are landing," he said. "Come right away." As there was not much snow in the fields, it did not take me long to run down to where the great X-12 had landed, in the same old spot. Frank and Frances were standing in the door-way, all smiles. "Christmas greetings old man" said Frank. "Come in, we have a surprise for you." "What do you mean 'Surprise,'" I said, "Is not your un-expected visit surprise enough?" "Well," said Frank, "we have a greater surprise. Come with us." So I followed them up to the top level of the great Space-Ship, which by means of the wonderful 'thought' operated life took only a few seconds, and there we were, almost 300 feet high. "Take a look Arthur," said Frank pointing to a large silver ball. "What is it?" I asked. "Looks like an over grown foot-ball, a silver Ball."

Frank laughed, and replied, "That foot-ball as you call it, my good friend, is a TIME MACHINE." "No kidding," I said. "No," replied Frank, "I am not kidding, that is a real Time-Machine. Would you like to go places in it? Back or forward into the past or future history of your world?" I was amazed, and only partly convinced. I had read many stories of Time Machines, very inter-esting but none of them true. But up to now I had no reason to doubt the word of Frank, and from beholding the wonders which I had seen on Venus, and the fact of this great Space Ship operated by thought alone, I knew that unless Frank was just pulling my leg, the Time-Machine was another wonder of Venus. I said as much to Frank. "O.K.," said Frank, "tell me, where do you wish to go?" "I would like to see what our world will be like two thousand years from now," I said. "For instance, what will my property look like? Will it remain a nice country place? I have ideas of what the world is rushing into so if your Time Machine really works, let's go." Without further remark, Frank open-ed a small door in the side of the great silver ball. "Are you ready?" asked Frank. "I am almost scared to death," I replied. Both Frank and Frances laughed at my amazed face. "No danger," they both assured me. "Just tell us where you would like to go. That is, have you made up your mind? Do you wish to go forward, or go back into history? To what year exactly, and exactly where on earth?"

"Well," I said, "if you are not pulling my leg, I would like to see my property, this exact spot, on the 24th day of December, 2000 years ahead from now." "O.K., said Frank, "go inside, sit down, and do not move at any time - remain in the exact same spot. But if you feel yourself to be in danger, or for whatever reason you wish to return, call out, or as you say on earth, 'Yell.' We will bring you back just as soon as we hear you." Without further words, I sat down and Frank closed the door leaving me in almost total darkness. Then a slight buzzing started. After what appeared hours, but really it was only a few moments, I found myself seated alone, and after a few seconds for my eyes to get used to the bright light, I noticed there was no snow, and the thing which I noticed most was the very warm temperature; in fact it was hot. But, I thought, how could this be? For when I had walked to the Space Ship on the 24th day of December 1969, it was about 25 below zero at Lake Beauport, not much snow, but we did have a couple of inches. Now here was I in exactly the same spot, with no Space Ship in sight, seated on a block of stone, outside in the open. Yes, it was hot. But, I thought, if this time machine is a fact, this was the year 3969! The world had passed through 2,000 years, and what a change! That which had been a tree covered mountain in 1969, was completely covered with ruins, no sign of any buildings, only ruins, block piled on block, no trees at all.

Was I dreaming? Was the Silver-Ball Time Machine a Fact? WHAT caused this ruin? Many questions passed through my mind. Large stone blocks, crumbling ruins, reminded me of pictures I had seen of the ruins of old Rome. Some day in the past, great stone buildings had been built on what had been my farm property. What caused their destruction? As far as the eye could see, complete total destruction; where was the once beautiful country gone? I sat there with sadness in my heart. There did not appear to be any life - no birds, or any little wild friends, who once used to come to meet me when I walked down into the woods. The ruins appeared completely dead, as far and in every direction the eye could see - nothing but ruins. I appeared to be free of the Silver-Ball, as I saw no sign of it. I was sitting on one of the stone blocks, and I could see in all directions. I did not dare to move because Frank had warned me not to, so I remained in the one spot. No life did I say? What on earth is that? Did my eyes play tricks? For there coming out from a space between large stone blocks, was a queer looking monster. It appeared to be about 50 feet long, with a large head, and all the appearance of a large lizard. It saw me and started to approach. It came within 100 feet and sat up! It looked funny, but I did not laugh. I wondered should I yell and let Frank bring me back to 1969, or should I wait to see if the monster came nearer? I also wondered, who was more scared, me or the monster? No doubt it had never seen a human creature before. Well, it did not appear interested in me, for he (or she?) soon got tired of watching me, and got down on all four feet, and started to eat some weeds growing between the stones.

All this time I had been wondering if the people who had built this place had left any records, and if so, how could I discover them? This was a problem because Frank had warned me not to leave my seat. I could see many stones of all shapes and sizes, perhaps someone had cut some form or kind of record into one or more of the stones, such as we do with a corner stone, but unless I could move from my seat, it would be impossible to find any record. There did not appear to be anything which I could do until I returned to the year 1969, and perhaps, interest Frank to return with me so that we could search for records. I was thinking along that line when I saw the creature, whatever it was, run back into the space between the stones. Something had scared it, but at first I saw nothing except the rocks. Then I looked up as I noticed the creature was doing, and in amazement I saw something was gliding down from the sky! Nearer and nearer it came, slowly it came and grew larger and larger until it almost covered the sky! "A space ship," I cried in amazement. Yes, indeed, but what a space ship! It appeared to be at least four times the size of the X-12. At first I felt like running, but something told me to remain where I was.

At last the giant ship came to rest. The control tower, made exactly like the X-12, was roughly 250 feet in diameter, and I figured it would be 900 feet high! The body of the ship covered everything in sight, it was roughly 2,400 feet in diameter. As I sat there, almost frozen with fear, the door opened - can you guess who came out? Yes, with a boyish grin, it was Frank, not looking a day older than when I had left him 2,000 years ago! Laughing at my surprised look he asked, "Why are you surprised? Did I not tell you that we of Venus live for thousands of years?" "Yes," I replied, "you did, but I am hard to convince. Is Frances with you?" "Yes, right here," said the silver voice of our beautiful friend as she came to the door, also not looking a day older. They both came and sat on the stone blocks with me. "Well Arthur," said Frank, "have you seen enough of the future?" "Yes and no, Frank," I replied. "I have a few questions, first how can I search these ruins? I would like to find, if possible, some record perhaps cut into the stones: try to find out what caused this ruin. Can I leave this seat or will you tell me the answer to this problem?" Frank looked thoughtful. "It is impossible for you to leave your seat, even for a moment without danger. But I will search for you," he said.

He then walked towards a large group of stones, and started to search, moving from stone to stone, and writing on a pad which he carried. It appeared to be hours before he returned with a smile on his face. "You found something?" I asked. "Yes," replied Frank, "I found something, not a complete record, I fear, but we have the sad story." "Sad?" I questioned, "just how sad?" "Well," said Frank, "I will try to give you a good picture of the past 2,000 years, according to that which I know personally, and from the records cut into these stones. It was during the late 1970's , between 1971 and 1978, that an Atomic war broke out between China and Russia. This led to the third world war; America, Canada, England and South America included. In the end no one won, as could be expected; most of the known world was almost completely destroyed, only a few persons who lived in the hills, and close to the North and South Poles managed to keep alive. The whole nature of Earth changed: the very seasons altered. The only people left were those of the hills of China, good people who had little use or need of those things which most of the western world depended on for their existence. It was (according to the records cut in the stones) in 1983 that the people of China moved to Canada, and the ruins which you see before you are a part of their development which continued until the year 2,920. In other words, the Chinese people owned most of the world at that time. Then without warning, the end came. One moment the people were doing everything they liked to do and worshiping the Sun-God. The next moment, all was destroyed, the Sun-God could not save them. As we read in the book of Revelation, there is but one God."

Frank continued, "The world of 2,920 thought they were above God. They had invented a super-system, as they thought, to maintain their material lives 'for ever.' They had no use for the God of love, they had completely forgotten the Atomic war of 1978. And then, the blow fell. The Astronomers had seen; had been looking at a bright red something for years. This something turned out to be a large ball of fire, and as it approached closer to earth, it was seen to be much larger than earth, and a good deal 'hotter.' In fact it turned out to be a ball of Atomic-Energy, but as it had been seen for ages, the world took it for granted. It was said to be 'just another bright star' until! -- the blow fell. The chief Astronomer at Montreal saw something new; the ball of fire seemed to be closer, in fact it appeared to be falling to earth fast! During the next few days many other Astronomers saw the same thing. Of course, the world at large said funny things about the old men who look at stars, but the ball of fire was getting larger, any fool could see that. But they had seen these comets before. After all, people were too wise to believe in God. Science said nothing like that could happen in this modern world - who was fool enough to believe in a god? So at last when the world Astronomers combined their findings and said the ball of fire would hit the earth very soon, no one believed, except the small handful left of that old group of fools who said they were 'Christians.' Of course, they were a laugh!

"Finally, after a few months of having fun with the silly Christians, the heat from that ball of fire was felt all over the world; the ice caps at the north and south poles were melting, causing floods, shocks were felt, rivers started to dry up, and in a few months no large steamers could pass up the great St. Lawrence River. The world leaders started to think,'well maybe the Christians had something after all, they appeared to be the only people left on earth who could still smile! But what was wrong with our boys of science who had told the world thqt this ball of fire was just a bright light, no danger!' The Hot Ball of Fire drew closer, no one could find a cool spot. Most people had fled to the Arctic, but it was even hot there. There appeared only one thing to do; get off the earth fast, but how could several billion persons leave? There was not a space ship to be had, and no time to build one, even if they knew how, but of course no one believed in space ships, any more than they believed in God. The end came quickly, shock after great shock hit the earth, and there was no place to hide, even the large caves inside the earth were destroyed, not one stone standing on another, a great big pile of rubbish: ruins, ruins. The few Christians were moved to the planet Venus, and returned to earth many years later, to start a new world, with God.

"And that," said Frank, "is the story of the end of the people of earth, according to my personal knowledge, and the records cut into these rocks. The records were made by the last people to live, a few months before the world was destroyed." "But," I asked, "what was this thing seen by the chief Astronomer?" Frank looked at me with sad eyes. "It was the 'Red Planet.' The people of earth were completely destroyed by the Atomic Energy transmitted from this planet when it came within reach. Man, by means of his foolish science, had destroyed himself. You see my friend, no one can live apart from God forever. God did not destroy them. This is not new, as I have repeated so many times in my message to the earth people. You never appear to learn by your mistakes, your great scientists appear to believe they know everything, and because in reality they know nothing, they bring destruction on themselves and all who have faith in them. Science under Divine Control is good, but without His will, it is evil." With those last words Frank said "Good-by." Frances waved her hand, and walked into the great X-12, leaving me alone with my thoughts, and many questions I would like to ask Frank. I then yelled, and found myself within the silver-ball, and in a few seconds, Frank opened the door, I stepped out, back again to Christmas Eve 1969! "Welcome Home," said Frank. "Tell us all the news." I told them all I had seen; the ruins, the monster, the giant space ship, and the story he had told me.

Frank and Frances were sad. "But," said Frank, "is it not true that your world has been warned for generations? The people of earth are working to destroy themselves by their foolish ways. God made one race of mankind, some red, some black, some of other colour--but all one race; need we tell you that you judge others because their skin is different, or because others have more, or less money, or perhaps their 'social background' is different! It is little wonder you have war and other problems. We still believe the earth man, in general, to be mentally ill; we have great difficulty of convincing ourselves that sane persons would behave as earth pecple do.

"In our first message we told you of our surprise to see the people of earth running around like insects, doing little of practical or constructive use, but just living as play boys, for self. Most of you end your lives sadly; even at this moment your nations plan to murder each other, watching to see who can throw the first atomic bomb, to blast the other, if possible, without getting hurt. You in Canada have the highest standard of living on earth, and in what manner do you thank God? It would appear from their actions, that the people do not appreciate their lucky position. From what we see, none of the earth people are satisfied with the good life, world conditions in this age appear to be the same as they were before the great flood; when every one except eight persons were destroyed. The people of that day were almost the same as the people of earth today! They were very religious, but worldly, materialistic minded. Note that before the flood, they had about the same 'new' morality as you have on earth at this time, and that is the reason for our coming in large numbers. You will note that the people before the flood were laughing at the few who saw signs, laughing at the silly old man building his flying-saucer (Arc), no one saw the signs. Note today, very few see our space-ships! Yes, the majority laugh, for as Christ said 'There are none so blind as those who refuse to see.' Only those who believe can see further than their nose, and that is why you saw ruins."

With these words Frank ended his talk, and Frances said she would give us a little talk for us to meditate on. "I will not say very much Arthur," she said. "We must leave, but we shall return soon, and at that time I will bring you another meditation. Here are a few thoughts about 'Visions.' Have you ever considered,my dear Arthur," she said, "that God's truest servants have lived by the power and guidance which came to them through their 'Visions,' while they looked not at the things which are seen, but at the things which are not seen. To most people, Venusians and your people of earth, and those of other worlds, glad and happy days come from time to time. Let us remember to keep our eyes and hearts open, to drink in all we can of joy in what we see and hear, during those glad days. It may come true even for us, that God should be with us in our gardens, and that we may learn to know Him better through the things that are made. But, how may we keep this spirit of life and light with us when the days darken again, and the shadows fall so early? Have we any inner vision which is not dependent on the various happenings of our lives? What can make us brave and quiet in grievous anxiety? What can steady us when the cloud of depression and sickness comes to us? What can calm us when the deep dark shadow of death falls on our homes and takes with it all our joy? What can give us patient wisdom with, and loving interest in, the children, old and young, according to their need? What can inspire us with understanding and love for all creatures? You know the answer, the world knows the answer. Your world trouble is the direct result of your rejection of the simple truth, as taught by Christ. Anticipating this rejection of idealism, of the true idea of God, this salvation from all error, physical and mental, Jesus asked, 'When the Son of man cometh, shall he find faith on the earth?' " With these words my Venusian friends bid me goodby, leaving me with the greatest truth, and wonder of my life.

I expected wonders. I saw a miracle.

# Chapter 8

After the great X-12 had left Lac Beauport on that cold morning of 1969, Frank sent the following message which I received on the Tesla-Scope:------

"The people of your world are on the verge of being wiped out by a cataclysm, as the result of the approaching armageddon, whereby combatants and civilians alike will be blotted from the face of the earth if something is not done to stop the present methods of evil and hate, which appear to be spreading all over the earth!

"Only sensible recognition of all national and individual rights of all people, and the right of all people to live in accordance with God's law will avert this cataclysm.

"The wholesale building of destructive engines of war will not save the world; and is only the method of lunatics who have lost faith in God. It is the right and duty of all sane thinking people to deliberately and definitely think of Him, and peace. All of the people on earth, each one of you, will be responsible for every life lost. It is not so much of what you do, but that which you do not do - for good, as you may read in the third chapter of Revelation. Each one of you will be held responsible if you do not do your utmost to prevent hate, or war. Engines of war, which is murder, are not required to prevent war. If you expect God to help, you must keep His law. If you keep that thought in mind, your problem will be solved. But to have peace, we must have peace in our hearts, for that which we receive is the reflection of our own desire, even if we do not know it. No one can deceive God because He can see into our hearts. In the past, from that which we see of you, the world has always been ready to blame God, or bad luck, or even to say 'There is no God' because He did not prevent sickness, death, and war, or to save you from the results of your sins. How can you expect Him to help you, when you only pretend to keep His rules or to even say that He did not give you enough strength to keep them?

"Therefore the answer to all of your problems, is to be honest with yourself, give up your foolish lust for personal wealth and power. Take a look at your history, where are all the great people? Where are your war lords? You know the answer. Is there any future for all those dead earth people? Did they take their silly power and false pride with them? Was their lust for power worth while?

"If the millions of people on earth were to wake up and put Christian leaders to govern them, using only the law of God, the results would be peace and happiness for all.

"According to the sixth commandment, "Thou shalt not kill." The true meaning of this has been rendered by Christ in His Sermon on the Mount, which you may read in the book of Matthew, Chapters 5, 6,7. Some people try to make themselves believe they are not guilty of murder, because they have their own personal meaning of the law. Blinding yourself to the truth does not make you one bit less guilty. Entering into, or encouraging of wars, or the envy of others, to hate or to dislike, to control by the force of will, to hunt for sport, to kill anything, to destroy any good desire on the part of any one, it is all murder. As Christ said, angry and evil passions are the seeds of murder. Cain first envied his brother, and after that he murdered him. The Pharises first hated Christ, and after that they were the means of His being put to death. Christ our Saviour not only did not go about wounding and injuring men, and putting them to death, but He went about befriending them, and doing them good, and we must, according to our opportunity, go and do likewise.

"Let us all reflect also, that when one thing is forbidden in scripture (and common sense), the thing contrary to it may be considered a command, in other words do the positive. 'Love worketh no ill to his neighbor,' therefore love is the fulfilling of the law. Do we then feel a tender concern never to hurt any one by word or deed? Do all earth epople consider it as a part of their business in life to support the weak, to feed the hungry, to clothe the naked, according to each ones ability, and also to comfort them that are afflicted, to heal the wounds which others give, and to all without thought of receiving thanks, and to remember that our own neighbor does not mean just our own kind, our own race, colour or country? It is a silly excuse to say we go to war because we must have more territory, for expansion; no country needs expansion. Your earth is supposed to be free to all who wish to live in peace and good will."

End of Message.

# Chapter 9

Some weeks after receiving the message from Frank, which he sent to me soon after the great X-12 had left me on that cold Christmas morning of 1969, I again heard the alarm sound on the Tesla Scope. Another message, I thought. Yes, sure enough, it was Frank. This time with a startling suggestion, to use his own words. "I wish to suggest that you come with us, on our next trip to the planet Mars! If you agree, we shall come for you sometime around March 9th." End of message.

A trip to the planet Mars! The mystery planet was there life as we know it on the "Red" planet? Frank did not mention anything about special equipment, no doubt he would supply it if it was required. Of course, I asked myself a lot of questions. Mars was far away. We knew now that man could go into space, because just recently a man had landed, and walked on the Moon! Not so far away from earth as the red planet, it at least proved the possibility of going to the other planets at some future time, but it will need something far better than a rocket! So during the weeks that passed, I did a great deal of thinking, and managed to make up my mind to accept Frank's invitation. The only things I knew about Mars were all pure theory, no one on earth could be sure of anything concerning anything outside of our world, and after all, we did not know all, or everything about our own earth! At last March 8th came and with it, my long wait for news from Frank.

Perhaps you are wondering what kind of ship we had? No need to wonder, it was the Venus Space-Ship X-12. Frank had long ago suggested that we might pay a visit to Mars. March 9th turned out to be an almost perfect day for take-off. I waited for the alarm to sound on the Tesla-Scope, again I had no sleep during the night of March 8th, but at last the alarm sounded at around 2 A.M. I again ran outside, in the hope I might see it landing, but there it was, at the same spot. I walked up to the door where I was welcomed by Frank and his charming companion, Frances. "Welcome old chap," they said. "This will make history for you," said Frank. "Yes, indeed," I replied, "Mars has always been an interesting subject, but few if any earth people believe there is life, as we know it, on that planet." "Wait until you arrive there," said Frank. In the meantime, the great X-12 was far above earth, which now appeared as a beautiful star, from so far away. The X-12 picked up speed, What speed! No earth man can imagine, contrary to all earth-science theory, the X-12 at such a speed, should have been completely destroyed, for it was moving 27 times the speed of light! At this speed we should reach Mars in about one-hour, allowing for slow-down at the half-way mark, and the landing. It was around 4 A.M., earth time, that we landed on the surface of Mars. Naturally, I was tremendously excited. I had looked forward to a possible trip to the red planet ever since our first visit to Venus on the X-12. Now here was I standing on the surface of this mystery! What next?" I asked myself. As Frank opened the door, he told me to "go ahead Arthur, step out. You have the honour of being the first earth man, since Adam left here, to walk on Mars." "But," I asked, "will I be able to breathe? What kind of air is it?" I soon found out, yes, it was good air, better than on earth, here so far there was no smell of smoke; yes, it was clean fresh air. I felt no discomfort, Frank and Frances followed closely behind me, and we walked towards a large group of rocks, but what rocks! Some of them were about 45 feet in diameter, and thousands of them covered that which appeared to be, otherwise, a large field, and in the far distance were a range of hills. We walked up to the nearest large rock, which appeared to be almost jet black. Frank scraped away a layer of soft earth, and by so doing, disclosed something bright. "What is it?" I asked. "Looks like gold," replied Frank. "Gold!" I exclaimed. "Yes," said Frank, "it is pure gold, but to be sure, let us test it, shall we?" Of course I agreed, so we returned to the X-12 and obtained a test out-fit, something like the Tesla-Bridge, with which we soon proved the rock to be pure gold!

We then made a test of all the nearby rocks, and to our surprise, and delight all of the rocks in the field were indeed, solid gold. "Well," I remarked, "if we could bring that one big rock to earth, we would be the richest people on our world. There is more gold in that one rock (pointing to the 45 foot high monster) than in all of our world!" "O.K." said Frank with a grin, "So you wish to bring this rock to earth?" "Yes," I replied, "if it could be done, but as you know, it is not possible." "I do not know any such thing," answered Frank. "It is not only possible to transport all of this gold to earth, but I will prove it to you!" "Well Frank," I said, "I have every reason to believe you, but it is beyond my understanding, at the moment, just how you can do this. That is to move this heavy mass, which must weigh many times more than your great X-12! I cannot imagine how you can even place it into your ship. How long it will require to break it into pieces small enough to lift into your ship, even if you do lift them with a hoist through the hatch." Frank laughed, "No my dear Arthur, we will not move one piece either by hand or with our hoist. We shall first return to earth, and then, if you still desire to be the richest man on earth, we will bring it right into your field, without lifting one ounce. ....."

"In the meantime, let us have a look around this planet." I was amazed at what Frank had told me, but knowing of the many wonders which I had already seen, not only on this great space ship, but also on Venus, I knew that anything Frank said was possible. So I agreed that we should take a look around this planet, which I, at least, knew nothing about, except the little information from our earth scientists, which they thought they saw by means of a very distant view, through a system of lens. Because of what they thought they saw, we were taught (on earth) that life as we knew it could not exist on Mars, because, so they said, humans could not breathe the air, and so many other reasons, none of which could be proved. The findings of these earth scientists was all based on theory, of course, which could never be proved from a distance of millions of miles. Why, they were even mistaken in their findings about the moon which is only roughly 240,000 miles away! Well, be that as it may, and to prove that the earth scientists were all wrong, here was I walking on the surface of Mars, without any special equipment, breathing the air, and so far, meeting no monsters. The place at which the X-12 had landed was almost level, except for these large rocks and the distant hills, which looked exactly the same as the hills we see around Canada.

The nearby ground was covered with a deep green moss, which was very pretty; here and there were bushes, and a few large trees, which appeared to be some type of oak. It was a clear day, this early morning, a few birds appeard, small and very pretty blue birds, they were not at all shy, and came close to us as we walked towards the hills.

"Will we meet any of those people we read so much about" I asked, "mechanical men, with queer long legs?" Frank laughed, "Yes, those queer ideas were invented by earth persons who do not believe in the Bible story of creation. Otherwise if they used their heads and believed, they would not think of such nonsense. For as you know, 'God made mankind in His likeness.' Surely," Frank went on to say, "there can be but one likeness of God, therefore, if there are beings on this planet Mars, and other planets, they will be like you and me, naturally of many sizes and many colours.  But of course, we people of Venus have been on Mars many times in the past, therefore we know there are real people of flesh and blood on this world, and I feel sure we shall meet some very soon, not far from those hills which we see in the distance.  "Are they friendly?" I asked.  "Yes," said Frank, "as friendly as you are.  Love reflects love, on Mars as anywhere else."

We had been getting nearer to the hills as we walked along, and soon approached another group of large rocks which looked very much the same as the 'gold' ones, and there we saw in the distance that which appeared to be a town.  Sure enough as we got nearer we could make out buildings.  These were not like those on Venus, but appeared to be more like our buildings on earth, all shapes and sizes, but no roads until we came almost within this town, which was now about one mile away.  I asked Frank about the roads.  "The people here,' he said, "have no use for roads, which as you know are a great danger on your earth.  You will find good roads within the towns, but as you will see in a moment, they have no need for any roads between towns."

Then I noticed that which appeared to be a car coming towards us.  As it came near, I saw there were six persons in it.  The car appeared to glide a few inches above the ground, it had no wheels.  As the car came within reach, I noted the persons in it were all dressed in silk-looking clothes.  I could not tell if they were men or women; none of the six had any form of head covering.  The car came up to us and the six persons got out and walked up to us, each of them with a bright smile.  They all held up their hands with the palms outward, and sent us a mental message of welcome.  "Welcome to Frank and Frances of Venus, and to you Stranger."  Frank quickly made us acquainted.  "This is our friend Arthur," he said, "from the planet Earth.  Arthur is interested in the field of black rocks, and would like to know if he may take some of them to earth."  The six burst out laughing.  "Surely," the mental message came, "Earth Man Arthur is welcome to all those black rocks."  "Thank you, kind friends," said Frank, "on behalf of our friend Arthur."

The six Martians then invited us into their car, we all got in and drove towards the town, the car rode perfectly smoothly without any noise!  It appeared to glide over the ground.  In a few moments we were in the town which Frank said was named "The City of Light."  Our car came to a stop, and we all got out.  Frank said, "Every one walks in the city."  The roads were simply beautiful.  The six Martians led us into a chorus hall, where I was told the people remain for hours, even days and weeks in these halls, which fill the city, listening in a sort of stupor or trance to beautiful music; for music is the one great recreation of the Martians.  It would appear that gradually, under the influence of this musical immersion, a mentality seems developed, and the soul moves out of the concourse of listening souls, moved by a desire to do something, into the streets of the city.

The Martians call this 'the Act Impulse.'  From that time on the soul rushes, as it were, to its natural occupation.  Its mentality, aroused by music, becomes full of some sort of aptitude, and it enters the avenues of its harmonious activity as easily, as quickly, as justly as the growing flower turns toward the Sun wherever it may be.   Let me present to you the curious scene my eyes saw as we sat in the great Chorus Hall.  I say my eyes.  It is hard perhaps for you to realize what an organ can be in a creature, so apparently, as we are, little more than gaseous condensations.

You have seen faces and forms in clouds.  How often have we watched their changing.  It is the same way with Martian music.  I seemed to be in a great

alabaster cage enormously large and very beautiful. Its shining walls rose
from the ground and at a great height arched together. The front was a net-
work of sculpture, it held the rising rows of what seemed like ivory chairs on
which the motionless white and radiant assemblage were seated. The whole place
glowed, and this glow prevails throughout the City of Light. The music came
from a wonderful array of beings seated all around the great hall. I could
almost see the music, as if it was truly formed like clouds. After remaining
a long time in the chorus hall, Frank said that due to our limited time, we had
best move on, so we left the solemn, swaying music and stepped out upon the
broad steps which face the city. We stood amid a colonnade of arches; the
white shining columns rose around us to the high shining roof, before us a
long descent of steps, and beyond us and around on a softly swelling eminence
was spread the City of Light. It was a marvellous picture.

The City of Light is simple and monotonous in architecture, but its composition and its radiance quite surpass any earthly conception. The buildings
are all domed and stand in squares which are filled with fruit trees, low bush-
like spreading plants, bearing white pendant lily-like flowers or pink button
shaped florets like almonds. Each building is square, with a portico of columns placed on rising steps, a pair of columns to each step. Vines wind around
the columns, cross from one line of columns to another and form above a tracery
of green fronds bearing red flowers; a sort of trumpet honeysuckle. The walls
of the buildings are pierced on all sides with broad windows, filled it seemed,
with an opalescent glass. Avenues opened in all directions, lined on both
sides with these wonderful houses, which appear to be made of a peculiar stone,
veined intermittently with yellow, which has the property of absorbing and
emitting light. Another strange feature in these Martian houses was the hollow sphere of glass upheld above each house. It is a sphere some six feet in
diameter made up of lenses, enclosing a space in the center of which is a ball
of the phosphorescent stone. During the day the rays of the sun are concentrated upon this ball of stone, and at night the stored-up sunlight (energy)
is radiated into light and heat.

It was the close of a Martian day that we left the chorus hall. As we
emerged, as I said before, upon the broad platform with its colonnade of columns and arches we saw the city as the night drew on. Each house built of this
strange substance, which during the day had been storing up the sun energy,
now, as the fading day waned, became a center of light itself. At first a glow
covered the sides of the houses, the colonnade and dome, while the glass prisms
above them sent out rays from their seat of stored up energy. The glow spread,
rising from the outskirts of the city in the lower grounds to the summits of
the hills where the sun's last rays lingered. It became intensified. The
green beds of trees were black squares and the houses, pulsating fabrics of
light between them. The whole finally blended and a sea of radiance was before me in which the beautiful houses were described, the illuminated groves,
and like enormous scintillations, the blassy spheres above them. As the night
settled down the light grew more intense, more beautiful. I could discern the
opalescent glasses in the houses sending out their parti-colored rays, patching
the trees with quilts of changing colours, and far away there came, still un-
subdued by night, the continuous elation of music.

So we went down the steps into the city, and as we walked I asked Frank
to tell me something of the Martian world. "The Martian World," said Frank,
"is one country, very much like Venus. There are here no nationalities. The
center of the country is in the City of Scandor, quite removed from the City
of Light. Business is carried on as with you on earth, but its nature and its
physical elements vary. As you will see, there is a circulating medium, banks
and business enterprises. One prime element of difference is in the nourish-

ment and the area of population. The Martian lives only on fruit, and he lives only a few degrees on either side of the Equator. All the businesses that in your earth arise from the preparation and sale of meat, and all the various confections disappear here, and also all the mechanism of house heating and lighting. There are no highways, no railroads, but many canals, which form a labyrinth of waterways, and are fed from the tides of the great northern and southern seas. The business is largely agricultural, but in the cities the pursuit of knowledge still continues. There is, however, on Mars a much lessened intellectual activity than on the earth. It is a sphere of simplified needs and primal feelings exalted by acutely developed love of Music. Mars is the Music Planet."

We now approached the top of the broad hill on which the City is built, and came suddenly out into a square filled again in its park-like center with trees. From amid these trees rose a massive building, which I recognized as an observatory. The many round domes, as on earth, were unmistakable. We entered the building and found that it was illuminated by its phosphori-glass walls, and its cool broad halls and stairways were, in the soft light, very beautiful. But their wonderfulness consisted in the insertion upon the walls of illuminated plans and maps of the heavens. These miniature firmaments were all afire, so that each opening, carefully graded in size to represent stars of the first, second or third magnitude, was filled with a beaming point of light, and I walked in these noble corridors between reduced patterns of the universe of stars. We now reached the ascending stairway which we walked up slowly, past great celestial spheres which filled the higher hallways. We entered a large central space, furnished with ivory chairs, and a broad massive center table, also of ivory, curiously inlaid with particles of the strange rock which gave out a liquid light and imparted indescribable beauty to the carved ornaments upon them. The floor was dark, a leaden colour, lustrous, however, like black glass and made up in mosaic. Around the room were alcoves lit by lamps of the 'light' rock, and in each alcove a glove of a blue metal upon which were painted sketches like charts or maps. A chandelier of this blue metal was pendant from the ceiling, and in its cup-like extremities, arranged in vertical tiers, were round balls of the 'light-rock' glowing softly.

Wide windows, unprotected by glass or sashes, just embrasures framed in white stone which everywhere prevails in Mars, looked out upon the marvellous City, which thus seemed a lake of glowing fires, over which, rising and refluent waves of light constantly chased each other to its dark borders, where the surrounding plain country met the City's edges. The walls of this beautiful room rose to an arched ceiling which was inlaid with this wonderful blue metal, seen in the globes, designed in scrolls and waving ribbons, and just descending upon the walls, themselves in attenuated twigs and strings. The walls were bare and shining. How thrilled and awe-struck I became as I gazed around me, so many wonders on this planet and so little time to see it; we must move on.

We left this wonderful building and made our way towards the "Garden of the Fountains," which I was told lies over toward the great Halls of Philosophy, Design and Invention, whose domes and temple-pointed roofs of copper and blue metal I could easily discern. It covers over half a square mile of space. It is supplied with water from an enormous lake resting in the hollow of an extinct volcano, fifty miles to the east of the City of Light, at an elevation of 5,000 feet. A great conduit or water pipe, as we would say, conveys the water to the garden. The Garden is built actually upon piers of concrete and stone, connected by arches of brick, and through the subterranean chambers thus formed, the division of the streams is made, and there controlled. The whole

84

was designed by the great Martian artist, Hinudi. The garden is approached through a labyrinthine avenue made up of Palms, which on that side of the City seem to be plentiful and over these palms, in extraordinary profusion, the vines of the red flowered honeysuckle. You cannot see beyond the wall of green on either side in this winding way, and only as you gaze upward does the eye escape the imprisonment of its surroundings, where above the waving summits of the palms you see a lane of the bluest sky.

As you draw near to the end of this oscillating road, into the garden, the splash and roar of falling waters invades your retreat. And then suddenly as if a curtain had arisen or dropped to the ground, you emerge upon a great marble terrace of steps and before you is spread a forest of geysers distributed in entrancing vistas in a lake of tumbling and scintillating waters. The scene is amazing and transporting. Rushing jets of water are enclosed in hollow pillars of glass, whose lines are ravishingly combined in the separate clusters of fountains. The heights of these fountains vary from 150 to 200 feet, and they are arranged in a peculiar disorder, which however, conforms to an elaborate plan. The water rises in these colored tubes in green columns, then breaks into sheets and bubble-laden cataracts of spray above them, pouring far outward like blazing showers of little lamps in the full sunlight. Many of the tubes are inclined, and the ejected shafts of water collide above them, producing explosive clouds of shattered vesicles of moisture that float off or drop in miniature rains over the lake. It made a bewildering picture. The exposure of water in the great lake which holds these fountains is broken with waves and the tempestuous scene with the constant excitement of the rising and flowing avalanches of water creates feelings of abounding wonder. The marble steps extend around the lake, and behind them on all sides rises the wall of the palms, beaten into motion by the wind blowing ceaselessly.

Frank decided it was time for us to get back to the X-12. We bid good-by to the six who had first met us, and also to a great number of others as we walked the beautiful streets in this wonderful City of Light. Back on board the X-12, on our long TRIP BACK TO EARTH THE QUESTION IN MY MIND WAS THE GOLD ROCKS which the Martians said we could have. I was wondering, would we be coming back to Mars soon? And in what manner Frank would place that heavy gold in the X-12.

To my question Frank said "Think well about this large amount of gold. Will having all that in your possession keep you happy and in good health? Do you know anyone on earth who has millions of dollars who is truly happy, healthy and well? Consider it well my friend. The gold is yours if you wish to have it, but in my opinion, nothing can replace your present well being, your good health, and the joy you share with others. Therefore I want you to think the matter over until we arrive near to earth. Then, and only then, give me your answer." Frank then left me to my thoughts while he went about the great ship. It required deep thought. Few, if any, earth men had seen even one-thousandth part of the amount of gold in that big rock. As the owner of it, I would be the rishest man on earth. Did I really wish to be that rich? I will not trouble you with all my thoughts, except to say that I came to the conclusion not to have the gold!

When we came within a few miles of the earth, Frank and Frances came to talk with me. "Well," asked Frank, "have you made up your mind? Do you, or do you not, want that gold?" In reply I found it hard at first, but managed to say, "No, Frank, I do not want that gold, but I would like you to tell me how you expected to bring it to earth, if I had said yes?" Frank said "Good thinking Arthur, we are very pleased to hear you say that you do not want the gold, as for the means by which we can bring the gold to earth, if you desire I will show you. As it is still daylight, we will remain at this level, and during our wait, which will be several hours, we might just as well set up our machine, by which we can transport the gold of Mars right on to your property." Frank grinned at me as we walked into the workshop on the second level of the X-12. "In this manner I will show you that which I intended to do, if it was your wish to have all that gold, however we are more than pleased to know that you do not want it. But we shall, if you like, transport just a little of that gold, to prove to you that we could, if it was your desire, place all of it right in your field!" Frank gathered together an assortment of things, tools and materials, electrical parts, wire, condensers, etc., and with all these things, I helped Frank to build a machine, a queer looking thing, which I thought was a very large high-frequency generator, until Frank enlightened me to what it really was. "This," said Frank, "is the Tesla method of developing a micro-wave of great power. Thousands of electrical horse-power is by this means built into a tiny beam, of less than one degree in diameter. By the power which we have on the X-12 we shall operate this machine, when we land on your property.

The tiny wave, or ray, developed will be directed exactly to hit the desired rock of gold. This gold rock, now located on the planet Mars, will be our positive pole, then by meansof this Tesla device the power ray, or beam, will be reflected from the gold rock, that is the positive atoms, and directed towards this negative pole. The gold is now broken up into its microscopic elements and becomes united with the elements of the micro-wave and thus carried to the negative pole by means of the reflective elements of the power ray. The Tesla device is therefore a practical method of transmutation of solids, that is the extracting ore or metal from a distant body without intervening physical means." By the time we had completed the machine, it was late evening, the X-12 completed the trip, and we landed around 10 P.M. We set up the machine in our field, beside the X-12.

Frank applied the power and directed the Ray so that it would hit the gold rock on Mars, then driven by accurate clock work, the wave could be depended upon to retain the proper direction, when once set. The ray was thus aimed directly, as I have said, at the large rock of pure gold. With breathless interest I watched the proceedings of ;rank. The strain upon my poor nerves was such as could not have been born for many hours at a stretch! When everything had been adjusted to his satisfaction, Frank stepped back, and pressed a lever. The powerful atomic engine, which he had built a few hours ago, instantly responded. "The beam is set exactly in the center of the large gold rock," said Frank. Then we waited; a minute elapsed, two minutes! I could hear the beating of my heart - the engine shook the ground - three minutes! Four minutes! We were like statues with eyes fixed on the polished ball of silver, supported by means of a high metal frame-work, which had a polished rod curved over the top like a crane. This was in fact the pole from which the energy was transmitted to the golden rock on Mars. Five minutes! "At last!" I shouted. "Look! Look!"

The shining ball had become a confused blue in colour, and I violently winked to clear my eyes. "At last!" The silver knob again changed colour, what seemed like a miniature rainbow surrounded it with concentric circles of blinding brilliance. Then something dropped flashing into a dish set beneath the ball, another, and another, glittering drop followed, and another, almost before a word could be spoken the drops had coalesced and become a tiny stream, which as it fell, twisted itself into a bright spiral, gleaming with many shifting hues, then overflowing from the dish. The tiny stream gradually grew in size, faster and yet faster it flowed, an interlacing maze of rings. After the five minute start, we timed the flow at One-Ounce per minute. Frank said this could be speeded up to a much greater amount. Frank let the machine operate for another minute, then turned off the power and we placed the parts of this wonderful machine into the X-12. Frank and Frances bid me good-by with the promise of returning soon.

## Chapter 10

It was some weeks after the last visit of the great Venus Space-Ship, and my first journey to the Planet Mras that I heard from my Venus friends, then one night the alarm on the Tesla-Scope sounded. It was Frank with another suggestion; this time, an invitation to take a further journey to Mars, but not in person. Frank said Frances would transport me to Mars by means of her mental-projector. I agreed; I would indeed like to complete our journey, for I felt sure there must be many more interesting things to see. So it was arranged; they would again visit me, sometime in March. It was during the early morning of March 14, 1969 that the alarm again sounded. I did not waste any time getting to the X-12. They were all ready for me, Frank and Frances were at the open door, with bright smiles to greet me. "Good morning Arthur, come right in." Frances had her projector all set up. "Let's go," said Frank, "take a seat Arthur." I did so, and the next thing I knew, I was on the Planet Mars, walking along with Frank!

How wonderfully strange and exciting it all seemed! We walked to the large canal, hurried to the pier, and got into a small boat. It was a curious vessel which appeared to be made of white porcelain; broad and short, with raised keel, prow, and expanded stern, moved by some form of electric motor. A pilot took his place at the bow, and, under a canopy of silk, in the light of a setting sun, followed by the music of the City of Light, we passed the city, which even as we left it, slowly, in the descending darkness of the night, began to brighten with the light of the rock, and send upward its magic glow. "These boats," said Frank, "are not in common use on the canals. The larger boats which are used for transport are made of the blue metal. All the boats are propelled by explosive engines, except these small ones, which have an electric motor. The power used to generate the electric current is obtained from the 'Energy-Rock.' These porcelain boats are curious; their sides, prows, poop and stern are ornamented by coloured designs, which are burnt in when the boat is made, for these extraordinary boats are made in huge furnaces in one piece, like a jug, vase or bowl. This small boat is propelled by a screw of blue metal." Down the crowded canal we slowly moved, amidst the calling crews, the pleasant cheers, and beckonings of sight-seers; and back of us rose on its hills the City of Light, which as we passed still further away, and watched in the fading sunset, began to glow, and finally, to shine like some titanic opal in the velvet shadows of the night.

As we slowly moved into the undulating plain country, with its pretty towns and farm lands, it reminded me of our beautiful Eastern-Townships in the Province of beautiful Quebec. We saw solitary projections of rock as the stars stole urgently into the sky. The magic stone lamps began their soft illumination of the decks, while the sound of songs from people on the land came to us in snatches bewitchingly mixed with the strange odors of the beautiful flowers and grass, which grew along the sides of the canal. The landscape about us was wonderfully illuminated by the two satellites, Deimos and Phobos, which as is well known, were first seen (or perhaps I should say - were reported to have been seen) by astronomers on earth. Prof. Asaph Hall is said to have been the first one on earth to report them, in 1877. What a marvellous sight they presented, moving almost sensibly at their differing rates of revolution through a sky sown with stellar lights. The combined lights of these singular bodies surpassed the light of our earth moon, by reason of their closeness to the surface of Mars, while the more rapid motion of the inner satellite causes the most weird and beautiful changes of effect in the nocturnal glory they both lend to the Martian life. We were now sailing in a wide river-like canal, about a mile or more wide. On all sides the undulating ground, covered with cultivation varied with thick patches of trees, with here and there shining lights from towns and isolated homes, carried the eye onward to a rising hill country, beyond which, again, silhouetted against the shining sky where Phobos began to rise, mountain tops were just discernible.

Deimos, the outer moon, was already shining, and its pale, sick light imparted a peculiar blueness, impossible to describe, upon all surfaces it touched. Here was the phenomenon we witnessed with increasing pleasure. Phobos was emerging from a cloud and its yellow rays possessing a greater illuminating power, mingled suddenly with the blue beams of Deimos and the land thus lit by the combined flood of light from these twin lights seemed suddenly dipped in silver. A beautiful white light, most unreal, fell on tree and water, cliff, hill, and towns. It was a print in silver, and while we gazed in mute astonishment, the sharp shadows changed their position as Phobos, racing through the zenith, changed the inclination of its incident beams. The effect was indescribable. I walked the deck in an agitation of wonder and delight, a delicious drowsiness overcame me, and after a while I noticed the pilot was changed, his place being taken by another, and that we were approaching a ridgy or rocky country. I found my way to the white couch prepared for me, and sank into a deep and dreamless sleep.

The morning of the next day was clear and beautiful. Shall I ever forget that first approach to the mountains of Tiniti, where Tour and Neu, the villages of the quarries, are located. All day long the boat ran through a diversified country, covered with great hills of worn pebbles and rolling plains of what appeared to be sand. The canal passed through solitudes, where the silence was only broken by the cackling laugh of a crane-like bird, marching in lines along the banks, or perched like sleepy sentinels amid the outstretched branches of the trees. These wild and fascinating regions were often alternated by miles of bright plantations, radiant with the yellow leaves of the Teloiv, bearing its deep red pods, while avenues of palms, not unlike the royal palm of the Earth, led in long vistas to clustering groups of houses, and we also caught glimpses of little lakes.

I was interested in the Martian custom of public worship. Frank pointed out to me the churches of the people, they appear to be built of the magic-stone, high above the ground, and approached by encircling terraces of steps. Frank said he did not understand the Martian faith. There seemed, he said, little to understand about it, it was one national expression of the love of goodness and of beauty, but it was all directed to a source of infallible wisdom, power and justice.

At last we arrived at the entrance of a gloomy and stupendous gorge. It was the wonderful passage driven through the first area of igneous rocks before we reached the quarry country of the Tiniti. It pierced the dark and stubborn dike that rose in sheer walls 1,200 feet above our heads, and it seemed that the tide was carrying us into the bowels of the sphere. At that moment a loud report was heard, followed by another. Looking upward, Frank with outstretched hand said, "It was a meteor, a big one." He called to the pilot to stop the boat. A few of the attendants were grouped near us, and the loudly suppressed exclamations made me realize that these visitations were perhaps infrequent upon Mars. It was a meteoric shower, like our leonids in November, which I had seen many times at Lake Beauport. It rained pellets, or balls of fire, these phosphorescent trains gleaming spectrally, while a kind of half audible crackling accompanied the fall. Shooting in irregular shoals or volleys, they would increase and diminish, and recurrent explosions announced the arrival at the ground of some meteoric mass.

We continued on our way, and soon entered a wild, savage, almost treeless country; the bare gray or rusty and jagged expanses sloping up steeply from the edge of the canal, sparingly dotted over with gray bushes, and covered with an ashen coloured lichen. We moved for miles through the waste of a ruined world. The whole region had been the stage of great volcanic activity, and the broad plains excavated with deep pools that reflected their dismal, unten-anted borders in the black depths of unruffled water, spoke of meteorological conditions long prolonged and intense. It was a weird strange place, silent and dead. But amongst these vast ejections, these fossil craters were embedded masses of the rare self-luminous magic stone that made the City of Light. The canal passed along for miles in the depression between two folds of the sur-face. Finally, gazing ahead, there slowly came into view a huge, gaping rent in the side of the black and gray and red walls to our right, and a minute movement of living forms, scarcely discernible, revealed the first quarry near the little town of Tour.

As we drew nearer I descried a slant incline from the open excavation down which the blocks of stone were slid. They were brought to the surface by hoisting cranes, and just as our little boat glided to the dock, an enormous piece of stone was moving down the metal roadbed to the edge of the canal. Here we landed, and a crowd of people hailed us, and amongst them were many of the copper coloured northerners who work in the quarries. Their day's work was over, and they crowded around us with interest. They were good-natured, but quiet, and dressed in a kind of overalls that was made in one garment from head to feet. Frank pushed amongst them, followed by me. We made our way to a pleasant house, built of the magic rock, and covered with an almost flat roof of the blue metal. In this house we were recieved by the Superintendent of Quarries. The greetings were pleasant, and as the Superintendent spoke both French and English, we got along fine.

The rooms of this house were large square apartments, simply furnished with the white chairs, tables and couches I had seen in the City of Light, but on its walls were drawings of the quarry, the country, and groups of the work-men. Amongst the pictures were some wonderful large scenes of an ice country, and the lustrous high wall of a gigantic glacier. I pointed these out to Frank. He told me that to the north of the mountains lay the great northern sea, in winter a sea of ice, and that from continental elevations within it, glacial masses pushed outward, invading the southern country. In regions beyond there were fertile plains. Here were their settlements from which the workmen of the quarries had been brought, beyond this again lay the margins of the polar sea. Song and music closed the day and after eating the wine-soaked cakes which the superintendent offered us, we made our way to the white and simple bed-chamber.

The morning came, fresh and splendid. The air of Mars is so pure, vivid and dustless! We walked to the quarry mouth, Frank and the superintendent in front of me, leading the way. I stood looking backward every few steps, de-lighted to trace the broad river of the canal winding through the desolation for miles beyond. Then I noticed how rapid and effortless is motion in Mars. Volition is so easy and penetrating, the body becomes a mere plaything for the mind. Frank beckoned to me and as I looked where he was pointing, I saw just ahead, a great black object, about which a number of workmen were running ex-citedly like a swarm of ants. Frank said "You remember the meteor we saw last night, well there it is." Extended like a gigantic and deformed missile lay an iron meteorite, still warm. A crevice spread down into its interior, and it bore the pits and depressions of the terrestrial objects. It measured some four feet in length, and must have weighed many tons.

We continued our walk and soon stood gazing upon the receding roof of the great cavern, the heavy walls left like buttresses to hold up the overlying mountain ridge. The quarry extends far in under the ridge. We were to descend, but before we did so the superintendent led us to the summit of the ridge. From here, we looked at a distant land beyond the volcanic area, occupied by farms and villages. It seemed peaceful and attractive. Beyond this again we just discerned the shimmering surface of the great Glacier, the superb train of ice. We descended again to the mouth of the quarry, and here we mounted a platform, used for an aerial elevator. On this we were swung far out from the dizzy sides of the quarry, slowly sank through the shaft of air, then passed into the cooler shadows of the deeper parts, where the sun failed to penetrate. I cried aloud with delight, and the abyss shouted its salutation back. Still we descended, and soon saw back in the deep prolongations of the tunnel the shining walls of this phosphorescent cave. The method of quarrying is very much the same as used on earth in the marble mines.

The mines were very interesting, but time was pressing. Frank said we must leave and continue our journey towards the next town. We started from the great quarry once more on the nice porcelain boat. The sterile, sinister and yet marvellous region of lava beds, dikes and craters suddenly was passed, and the canal moved into the huge forest lands. This is a beautiful land: mountain ranges rising from four to six thousand feet cross it, holding broad valleys and plains, or elevated plateaus between them; lakes and rivers pass through it. The canals cross the great region in many directions. The trunk line we followed was carried up and down by systems of locks of astonishing magnitude and perfection. Great lakes were made convenient feeders, and rivers were also tapped to keep the water levels constant in the canals. The weather was that of a semi-tropical paradise, and the late flowers filled the air with fragrance. Quickly now we approached the great city of Heneri, and the pilot pointed out to us the distant hills, almost purple in a twilight haze, which encircled the Valley of the City of Heneri. The country we had entered was a fertile farm country, where great plantations and vineyards were established, and where great flocks of doves, are found. The enormous flocks of this snow-white bird were strangely beautiful. They made clouds in the air. Finally we came to the last tier of locks at the summit of which my curiosity was to be satisfied by a view of the great City of Heneri, the CITY OF GLASS.

It was night when our little boat floated upon the waters of the last lock that completed the ascent, and immediately below, the observatory station of Heneri. I was standing on the deck of our boat, watching impatiently the slowly rising tide upon which we were borne upward. Above us, looking at us with interest, on the walls of the lock, I could at first see, as we ascended the towers of the observatory station, a company of Martians. The night was clouds, and the lights of the hastening satellites were but intermittently evident. Gradually we passed upward beyond the obstructing wall and gate, and the wonderful and unimaginable splendor of the City of Heneri, like some great opal, lay before us in the immediate valley. The glistening panes of water below us marked the places of the descending line of locks. Around us were the buildings of the Heneri Observatory and to the right and left swept the forested slopes of a circular range which, as I later saw, ranged about in one amphitheatrical circuit, the great vale of Heneri. The wonderful city glowing below us seemed to magnetize attention, and control, through its wonderfulness, each wavering attitude of interest. The eye of earth man never beheld so astonishing a picture.  Imagine a city reaching twenty miles in all directions built of glass variously designed, interrupted by tall towers, pyramids, minarets, steeples, light, _fantastic_ and beautiful structures, all aflame, or rather softly radiating a variously coloured glory of light.  Imagine this great area of buildings, penetrated by broad avenues, radiating like the spokes of a wheel from the center where rose upward to the sky a colossal amphitheatre.  Imagine these roads, delineated to the eye by tall chimneys of tubes of glass through which played an electric current, which removed every trace of smoke, converting each one into a lovely pillar.

I could see canals or rivers of water winding through the City spanned by arches of flame, but the night was still further turned to day, for above the city, high in the velvet black sky were suspended thousands of glass balloons, each emitting the soft illumination that marked the lines of streets.  So full and opulent was the flood of light, that the summit I had reached, the encircling hills, and the farther side of the saucer-shaped valley where Heneri lay, were bathed in an equally diffused radiation.  But as if the heavenly marvel might still further startle and amaze and charm me, from the City rose the swelling chords of choruses; billows of sound, softened by distance, beat in melodious surges on the high encompassing lands.  I stood mute and transfixed.  It seemed a beatific vision.  If the very air had been filled with ascending choruses of angels; if the dark zenith had opened and revealed the throne of the Almighty; it would have seemed but a congruous and expected climax.  Long I gazed, then Frank by my side woke me up, as he said "Let us be going Arthur, there is plenty more to see and much to do."  We then continued to walk towards the city and had gone but a short distance when a messenger met us with an important message for Frank, who was to return with him to the Council!

The messenger was a beautiful youth, not dressed as the citizens of the City of Light, but clothed in a tight fitting doublet of a creamy colour, with short trunks of yellow, and on his feet were sandals.  He saluted me, and said, "Greetings Earth man, you may come along with our Venus friend."  "But," said Frank, "what do you require of me?"  "It is the Council who seek your service," answered the messenger.  "I advise haste.  There is great excitement and dread in Heneri, Mars is in the path of a comet!"  Without further delay we made haste towards the Hall of the Council, a low inconspicuous building of yellow brick.  The doors of the single chamber, which embraced all the interior space, swung open, and we stood on the threshold of a shallow, rectangular depression, surrounded on all sides with benches, and holding in its central area a long table, at which, beneath tall lamps sat perhaps a dozen men and women.  The faces of these rulers of Mars, for that is what they were, turned to us as we entered.  The messenger announced us, and we were invited to seat ourselves at the head of the table.

"Welcome stranger from Earth, we know Frank of Venus.  The Martian spirit is that of salutation and friendship.  We have heard of the discoveries made on Earth by your friend Tesla, which have led your earth people to journey into space, and warned you of the danger which now apparently is about to cause the doom of this great city, and perhaps destroy the planet Mars, which we are informed, lies in the path, certainly defined and determined by observers, of a large cometary mass, which will plunge upon it a rain of rock and red-hot iron.  Even now this approaching body grows more and more visible in the sky.

The astronomers are working at the problem, hoping some deflection, some interpositional mercy will carry off this disturbing incidence.  But if we are to be destroyed, if there is no escape from the singular fortune of annihilation by an inrushing stream of meteoric bodies, then warning through proclamation, shall be made, and our citizens will move out of the city, and go away from it as far as possible, in the hope that the whole of Mars will not be completely destroyed. We have no other solution, except it may well be, that our good friend from Venus, Frank, perhaps sent to us by a greater power, has the answer. This is our last hope. We therefore give to you the power to direct us. Whatever you say will be done. Take time to think deeply before you decide that course you wish to follow. In the meantime, you shall be the guest of our City, and if it must be that this great capital of Mars must succumb to this mysterious invasion; if this place, so long a marvel of beauty, shall be succeeded by a heap of burning stones, then you shall be our companions in pilgrimage. Please remain with us until the end of this strange circumstance is known."

As he finished a noise of indescribable lamentation from a multitude of voices broke upon our ears, the sound of running feet and sharp cries of amazement, crashed in upon the half ominous silence about us, and then, the doors of the room swung open, and loud voices were heard crying, "The Peril comes. Run to the Hills!" Panic, that nameless mental terror of the unknown, which on Earth spreads fever-like through multitudes, had arisen amongst the Martians, and hurrying crowds were hastening in a wild retreat from this wonderful City of Glass to the hills. It has always been the same. When man places his faith in man made Gods he finds out the hard way that he has no place to go. As at the time of the flood; millions ran, but they found no place safe to run to, so it was on Mars. It had placed its faith in man made beauty! Well, here was something they could not face, so, as on Earth, they ran!

Frank looked thoughtful, he took my arm and we walked outside, Faces were turned toward the sky, the approaching thing had grown sensibly since an hour ago! It glittered, and now appeared to be the size of the full moon, and a light coruscation seemed coming from its edges. The fears of the multitude were justified. The mass above us was a train of missiles, hurling toward Mars! Its contact seemed more and more imminent. I felt a nameless terror, for a moment only; for when I turned to look at Frank, I saw that he was not a bit troubled. "Frank," I said, "are you not afraid of this mass of "something," which is about to destroy this City, and perhaps the planet Mars?" Frank looked at me, with a smile, and replied to me with a question, "No Arthur I am not worried and you should not be. You pretend to believe in Christ, you say you believe in the one great God. Your present action will prove if you are a Christian or not!

Remember, your world was destroyed by water; millions at that time pretended to believe in God, they went about doing good, that is, good according to them, but when that great test came only eight persons could prove they really believed in God, and therefore they were saved. If you my dear Arthur, believe in God, that thing above which you appear to be afraid of can not harm one hair of your head. The people of Mars have a lesson to learn.

Let us return to the council room." We found the members still at the table, they invited us to join them, which we did. Frank then said; "Friends of Planet Mars, I have carefully thought over the matter, and by the special Thought Power which we use on Venus, I have made contact with our rulers, and otherwise men and women, who assure me, and I am instructed to extend their finding to you, which I trust you will accept in the spirit of friendship and love, with which I give it." The Mars leader said that anything Frank said would be accepted in that spirit. "Thank you for this great honour," said Frank. "Our wise leaders tell me that the mass above our heads, will not destroy this great Planet Mars, nor will it completely destroy this city. I am informed that this object is sent to you as a last warning to mend your ways, throw away your false Gods, whom you note do nothing to save you from this thing which your people fear so greatly. You will not be offered a second chance, there is but one God; if you are wise, you will believe in Him."

With the ending of those words, Frank sat down. For many moments there was complete silence; no one spoke. Then the leader rose. "Thank you Frank, you have indeed taught us a good lesson. I must admit, we have forgotten God; we placed all of our faith in the material beauty which you see all around us. I will now inform the people of your message. You and your Earth Man friend have the freedom of Mars, do as you wish. Time will soon prove your statements, but before we part, will you tell me to what extent Mars will suffer?" "Yes," replied Frank, "the wise leaders of Venus say that Mars will never be completely destroyed; but some of the man made beauty, such as your glass buildings will be damaged, and some of your people will no doubt be hurt if they remain within the glass buildings. Soon, you may expect a shower of small stones, that is all." "Thank God for His mercy and goodness. With your permit Arthur and I will remain within this building of brick and its strong iron roof!"

Almost before Frank ended his talk, we heard the patter of rocks, falling on the roof. It grew dark, as if a thunder storm was over head. The shower lasted for almost two hours, then the sun came out, the patter on the roof stopped, and Frank and I walked out side. Where was the once beautiful Glass City? Nothing but a broken waste lay around, many feet deep of broken glass. What a sad ending, but it could have been worse. I must have said my thoughts out loud, for Frank answered, "Yes my dear friend, it could have been much worse, and now as we have seen this planet, let us return to earth. But before we leave we must return to the council room." We then walked back into the room, where we found the members still seated, looking at a large "living" picture, which was located on one wall. They asked us to join them in a picture journey around the planet to view the damage. To our amazement, we saw that every city on Mars had been damaged! But the leaders agreed with Frank when he said "It could have been worse." The people had a great lesson, they would rebuild, but this time it would be built on the solid foundation of Christ.

Afer we had seen all of Mars, we requested permit to leave, which the leaders granted. As we bid each other good-by, I was wondering how we would return to Earth. And when I asked Frank, he replied, "We shall return in the same way in which we came, when you are ready just say the word, and Frances will bring us back." I felt the same as I did when I first walked on the planet Venus. It was difficult to believe that it was only my mind here on the planet Mars. "All ready," I said to Frank, "lets get to dear old smoky earth," Frank then took hold of my hand, and the next moment we were in the great X-12, where Frances greeted us with her beautiful smile. "Welcome back home" she said. "Did you like Mars?" "Yes and no," I replied. We told her what had occurred, but of course she had seen it all on her magic projector, and then in a few moments it was time to part, I again watched the great ship float away into the misty sky

Chapter 11

Space ships were not unknown some two-thousand years ago, and long before that, for we read of many in the Bible. It is even possible to believe that Adam came to earth in a space ship! - we will go into that story later.

It also appears that Antony not only knew about space-ships, but actually used them in his war against Rome! This fact we read in a letter from Planous which he wrote to Cicero in the year 44 B.C. Planous (to Cicero) said, "Some occurrences have arisen since I closed my former letter, of which I think it may import the republic that you should be apprised; as both the commonwealth and myself, I hope, have reaped advantage from my assiduity in the affair I am going to mention.

"I solicited Lepidus by repeated expresses to lay aside all animosities between us, and amicably unite with me in concerting measures for the succour of the republic; conjuring him to prefer the interest of his family and his country to that of a contemptible and desperate rebel; and assuring him, if he did so, that he might entirely command me upon all occasions.

"Accordingly, by the intervention of Laterensis, I have succeeded in my negotiation; and Lepidus has given me his honour, that if he cannot prevent Antony from entering his province, (Narbonensian-Gual); he will most certainly lead his army against him. He requests, likewise, that I would join him with my forces; and the rather, as Antony is extremely strong in cavalry, and is said to have a great power from a somewhat unknown force, which appears to be a large bird like creature.

"This creature, which I clearly saw, flew very high above our heads, and in moments, by means of fire balls, destroyed a large part of our cavalry. We were forced to run towards the Isara, a very considerable river, that bounds the territories of the Allobroges." - End of quote from The Letters of Marcus Tullius Cicero.

Although most UFO sightings can easily be ascribed to honest mistakes made of natural phenomena and man made objects, there are no doubt many genuine UFO sightings which have been taking place all over the world, since I first received the visit of a very large something! I say "something" with good reason because at the time, that is to say during the second world-war, and remember this was in April 1941; therefore the "something" which landed in my field looked very much like a German air-ship! Without lost time I reported to the police that I thought an enemy air-ship had landed in my field. I had no reason to believe it was not an enemy ship until some time later when its crew sent me a message, which I recieved on the Tesla-Scope. Up to that date I knew little or nothing about space ships, but when I heard that message I became very interested and started to study everything I could obtain on the subject. My study led to the Bible, and Roman History, and many other old books. By the end of 1957 I had obtained a very good record.

It was not until 1947 (six years after I published my story) that world-wide interest (someone coined the word "Flying Saucer") started. Witnesses included reliable people representing all walks of life, from the highly trained scientist to the illiterate native in remote areas of the earth. All have described strange oval and cigar-shaped objects which, under many and varied circumstances, have behaved as if they were under intelligent control. After years of careful and conservative study, I am certain that there is more than ample high-quality evidence from trained and reliable witnesses to indicate that there are solid machine-like objects operating under intelligent control within our atmosphere. The wonderful performance of the objects, which I consider are the True Space Craft, rule out man-made or natural phenomena.

Such observational evidence has been well substantiated in many instances by reliable instruments, such as we used at Gagetown, N.B., last fall (1969), when several hundred persons saw the great Venus ship, the X-12. Even without the personal contact which I had with the X-12, my opinion, based on other evidence, is that UFO's are controlled by superintelligent beings from another world and have been carrying out a systematic program for reasons known only to themselves. There is no reason why other worlds do not know of our low type of culture, and the awful condition we have always been in; a culture of doubters and wholesale murder. Frank said during one of his visits, "No wonder you are backward. A world that believes in evolution is sick. Even a child should know better than to believe that God told lies. To believe in evolution would indicate that your people either do not believe in God, or else they believe He did not tell the truth, for He said that man was made in the likeness of God which means that He made Man Perfect. The crackpots who invented the theory of evolution, did so in their effort to destroy the peoples' belief in God, therefore, as your world appears to accept this foolish man-made theory as fact, your world is bound to be set back, or at least remain at a standstill until such time as you return to God."

The intensified program may have been instigated by the people of other worlds due to the fact that our civilization has reached atomic murder level, and is rapidly approaching its end; as we are told in the Bible, when "Stars" will fall from heaven. Therefore the presence of space-ships near our Earth might be one of great theological significance.

With the invention of modern astronomy man began to speculate on the possibility of life as we know it on other worlds. No one really knows what is beyond our sun; no one knows how many stars exist! - and if life, as we know it, does exist, it would mean that just within our galaxy alone, there could be a billion planets with civilizations of varying technology. Many of them might be thousands of years ahead of our "modern-world."

Angelo Secchi, the great Jesuit astronomer, asked the following question in the mid-nineteenth century; "Could it be that God populated only one tiny speck in the cosmos with spiritual beings? It would be absurd to find nothing but uninhabited deserts in these limitless regions. No, these worlds are bound to be populated by creatures capable of recognizing, honouring and loving their Creator." Yes indeed, I have every reason to agree with Angelo Secchi. The earth is too small a speck to fill the need of so great a God whom I love. If, as I suppose, there are unfallen beings in the universe; beings who have always obeyed Divine Law, such beings would advance thousands of years ahead of earth man, for it is our sins which have prevented our advancement beyond the lower creatures. It is a fact, and as it may seem that many of the lower creatures are far above man, look around you if you dare! What do you see? Most of the world devoting their time to bad habits.

From my personal study of the Bible and other books, and from what the crew of the X-12 told me, it became quite apparent to me that mention of space-ships is made in the Bible, and that these craft have visited our earth since the dawn of civilization. I would suggest that the reader search ancient records, including the Bible; one never knows - you may find something new. Take a look through the Bible book of Ezekiel. Chapter one is a clear description of an air-craft, as is also the story continued in chapter 10. Thus, in almost every Bible book can be found something about space-craft.

If these objects were space-craft, descriptions of them would be limited by the inability of the people of that age, to describe them except through the limited non-technical language of that day. Let us look at the language as used by Ezekiel Chapter 1, verse 4 - "And I looked, and behold, a whirlwind came out of the north, a great cloud, and a fire enfolding itself, and a brightness was about it, and out of the midst thereof as the colour of amber, out of the midst of the fire ----" end of quote.

The whole of this chapter from Ezekiel probably contains the finest description in the Bible of space-craft landing and of their crew, now let's take a look at Chapter 4, verse 22 and 23. "And the hand of the Lord was there upon me; and He said unto me, 'Arise, go forth into the plain, and I will talk there with thee.' Then I arose, and went forth into the plain; and behold, the glory of the Lord stood there, as the glory which I saw by the River Chebar; and I fell on my face." End of quote. What kind of glory of the Lord was standing in the plain, where the Lord talked with Ezekiel?

We read in Chapter One, that Ezekiel was sitting on the banks of the Chebar River when he saw the machine which looked to him like a whirlwind, so the glory which he mentions in Chapter 4 would be the landed craft! The whole Chapter 10 contains another wonderful account by Ezekiel of an air-craft, or space ship. Let's look at verses 4 and 5 - "Then the glory of the Lord went up from the cherub, and stood over the threshold of the house; and the house was. filled with the cloud, and the court was full of the brightness of the Lord's glory. And the sound of the cherubim's wings was heard even to the outer court, as the voice of the Almighty God when He speaketh."

Orthodox beliefs have for so long become almost indelibly ingrained in mankind today that I do not suppose anyone will accept the ideas which I have tried to illustrate in this book. But I write this for the few who are willing to do as Christ said, - "Open our eyes (and hearts) that we may see the truth, for there are none so blind as they who will not see."

In the early half of the sixteenth century the Renaissance was just flowering into the Reformation. Times were something like our own. In those days, the mere printing of the Bible for all men to read was an invitation to be murdered (in the name of religion). Many persons were murdered; either because they were caught reading it, or because someone thought they should read it. Today, in the so called "modern age," people are murdered because they differ from others in their beliefs. The writer and any others who dare to give an individual, unorthodox interpretation of the Bible, or parts of it, must be prepared to face an equal opposition; after all, was not Christ murdered because he dared to preach the truth! If the reader is surprised that I bring in the Bible and the religion of Christ into my story, he should not be, for the space-craft and true religion go hand-in-hand. One can not make a sinceree study of space-ships unless we wish to truly understand the will of God for man, for that is the real message of the people who come to earth from beyond.

Chapter 12

TRIBUTE TO NIKOLA TESLA - First Published In Newspapers 1943

The other day the most gifted man the world has known died, he left the world richer by over a thousand inventions that God allowed him to conceive. With the passing of Tesla I have lost a very old friend, and because of my intense admiration for him I write this modest tribute.

At the age of eleven, I had two teachers, Mother and Tesla. From her I learnt about God. Electricity fascinated me even at that age and my first reader was Tesla's investigation of high frequency currents, and I think I knew more about Tesla's inventions at the age of twelve than most enigneers do now. Not only did I know something about his wonderful ideas, but my brother and I actually built a working model of his wireless power transmitter, sending power without wires (using only the earth) from Quebec City to the Lavel hills, a distance of fourteen miles; this was in 1906.

And because I have lived and breathed Tesla the best part of my life, I know that his invention to end destructive wars (which he announced in 1934) would have prevented the second world war if it had been adopted. For if this idea had not been practical Tesla would not have announced it, because in spite of anything said to the contrary, he was never a wild dreamer. All around us we see proof of this. The new Shipshaw power system is one of Tesla's 'wild' dreams because it was he who invented the impossible thing of harnessing water power, and the hundred and one things, without which, no power generating and transmission system can operate. Most, if not all, of our electric light and power are operated by means of current supplied by machines of his invention; the alternating-current system including means of generating, transmitting, and using this energy. He invented and built the first and only practical motor that would run on the A.C. current.

It was characteristic of Tesla that he developed all of his ideas and actually built them to perfection before he announced them, and that is the reason I have always taken it for granted that anything he made public must work. I wonder how many realize that the progress of industry during the past forty-five years is due to the inventions of Tesla! It may be rather difficult to convince the average person, but the proof of this amazing statement can be seen all around us; a glance through the patent records, and a study of Tesla's articles proves him the inventor of many things that others are given the credit for. There are many men who have tried to take away the credit for the radio invention, but from records to be found in his many lectures and patents, it is proved without a doubt that he is the inventor.

Many well known engineers have, in the years since 1896, made various forms of wireless machines, one and all using the basic principles invented by Tesla. They all use his oscillator-transformer in one form or another, and have designed new parts all using the same basic idea. The perfect radio has yet to be made, and when it is, it will be a Tesla machine; the so called modern radio is not near perfect. In the future Tesla radio, all the power is sent from the transmitter. Tesla started his investigation of high frequency in 1889; he gave a demonstration of transmission of this current without wires through the earth in 1891-1892; he gave an outline of this work before the Franklin Institute and National Electric Light Association in 1893; he explained the plan to Prof. Helmholts with experiments, he stated it was practicable, and he perfected his system in 1896. In the summer of 1897 Lord Kelvin (whom my father worked for in England) honoured him with a visit in New York. He was carried away with the idea but at first condemned it because he thought it was Hertz waves, but approved when he was shown that it was true conduction, and was transformed into the warmest of supporters.

The basic idea of the Tesla system, used in every radio, is the oscillation transformer, consisting of capacity and inductance which may be connected and interconnected in two, three, or more circuits. Many interesting facts can be obtained from Tesla's patents which anyone can obtain from the U.S. Patent Office. In those patents can be found the formula to end wars, and to send power to any part of the world, and even to other planets, without wires. I believe that it was his idea when he obtained the patent of 1896, to send the power in electrical energy from Niagara, to any part of the globe, without loss.

This power in a slightly different manner is used to energize the war defensive barrier. In this machine the energy is concentrated and built up to an enormous amount. It then projects electrical controlled particles, enabling the conveyance to a great distance of thousands of horsepower, which nothing can resist.

Others have devoted considerable time, seeking a practical apparatus similar to that of Tesla. It is not surprising that they have not found it, because the majority of professional scientists are tied down by hard and fast rules of out of date theories, so that it is only on rare occasions, more often by pure chance, that a new principle is discovered. Tesla, on the other hand, made his own theories and proved them by practical demonstration. There had always been a strange antagonism towards Tesla, chiefly because he was so glaringly straightforward and honest; he made fools of experts who said "It can't be done" by doing the impossible. Tesla gave the credit for his ability to discover astonishing new principles to his Maker, who gives this rare knowledge to chosen individuals, who are thus ordained by Him to help mankind overcome some of their difficulties.

# Chapter 13

## TESLA'S INVENTION FOR DEFENSE BY ELECTRICAL ENERGY

We know what the 'scientific' world thought about Nikola Tesla's statement which he made in 1934, that he had discovered a 'new' principle which made it possible to transmit an electrical force, in a beam (not a death ray), of infinitesimally small cross section, something close to one millionth of a square centimeter.

Because of its attitude towards anything new from Tesla, the scientific world lost (for a time at least) the secret of this new principle. One of the keys to it is in Tesla's statement, "There is no energy in matter other than that received from the enfironment." As I am writing this for the benefit of the man on the street, it would be well to state that electricity is the old-fashioned name for the thing which makes your Radio, T.V., etc. work, and lights up the world, and this new Tesla discovery is just another electrical machine. During his life time, Tesla had discovered, invented, and built many wonderful machines, among which are the Radio, Radar, T.V. and MANY OTHERS which I have already told you about.

In a letter which I received from Tesla in 1932, he said that he had made an extraordinary new discovery, the key to which can be found in the Bible (Revelations), making it possible to send an electric current of very small cross section, through the earth, above the earth, and under the sea; also to flash considerable amounts of energy through interstellar space to any distance without the slightest dispersion. This narrow beam is the secret of perfect T.V. of the future, also of Radar, and long distance telephones. By its use we can do away with the aerials, poles, towers and micro-wave reflectors, etc. Also by its means we can communicate with the planets, and, very important, provide power to operate a space ship, which is a big step from the rockets which blast one's head off! It eliminates the need to carry fuel, leaving more space for the pay load.

What is the secret of this discovery? How does it work? In the DEW line for instance, we have a line of stations, each one of which could be blasted off the earth. In the Tesla system there are no 'visible' material stations (poles, relays, etc.). Instead we peak the beam, in standing waves, at pre-determined intervals. The 'peaks' rise above the earth, or over the earth, at right angles to the feed wave (or beam). The peak can go up any distance which is a radius of the earth, from the transmitter to each peak, the beam, wags back and forth, or revolves around the earth at a predetermined speed of from one to 24,000 times per second. In doing this, it sets up secondary (or induced) currents. Any object coming within a peak (or beam) WILL CAUSE SAID BEAM TO INDICATE THE FACT, which is felt at the transmitter station. The position of the object is thus seen, and can, if necessary, be destroyed, by means of the same peak or others.

Tesla's machine, therefore sets up millions of invisible towers all over the world, under and above the land and sea, so nothing can pass or exist without detection, and by its peculiar action, a war head can be destroyed before it has time to leave home. This machine is therefore the answer to the murder rockets. How does it work and who will be the first to build it? The Soviets, or any one who can use their heads and read, might know how it works because the secret of its operation can be found in Tesla's lectures. The scientific world ignored Tesla, and certainly, the western world ridiculed his most important ideas. Tesla once said "The walls of Jericho were made to fall through vibrating energy, directed against them by men who in tune with God, were skillful in the use of intensely simple machinery, but wonderfully effective, and I believe most firmly that when we come to know a little more than we yet know of how to manipulate the force of SOUND, we shall literally remove mountains through an application of the law of vibration. I do not regard the Bible narratives as myths; they are to me a scientific revelation, dim in places, I grant, but nevertheless, storehouses abundantly filled with the vast knowledge accumulated by the Godly and truly learned in ancient times. In the future, men and women who are truly in tune with God will continue to discover wonderful new inventions in the Bible put there by divine will for the good of mankind.

# Chapter 14

Copy of my notice published in Quebec City newspaper, January 2, 1939.

"Concerning the strange Air-Craft which appeared at Lake Beauport, Quebec, Canada, at 2 O'Clock in the morning of Tuesday, December 27th, 1937, the drawings shown are made from marks left on the snow, by a very large object, which for the want of a better word, I name an "Air-Craft." Because of the all too brief a glimpse which I had of the strange craft (and almost total darkness), my discription is mostly surmise. But the size of the machine is based on actual measurements taken immediately after it's departure. It is possible the machine is an experimental Blimp, or Air-Ship, that is in fact one reasonable explanation, which, however, does not explain it's speed, lack of noise, or the mysterious power which can make people unconscious at a distance! Another explanation of the craft, which is not so feasible, is that it comes from outer-space, perhaps the planet Mars, or Venus! CERTAINLY it's mode of propulsion must be new, otherwise the craft would have been detected by the sound of the usual motors or jets as used on our air-craft. The only reason which made me aware of it, is the fact that I have erected on my property, a Tesla Intruder Alarm. This instrument, which I have built from information outlined by Dr. Tesla, detects the intrusion of any object which comes within it's working radius, which is adjustable to close range, or a great distance. My present testing apparatus consists of a 75 foot pole, on which is fastened a metal plate, the surface of which is sensitized, and by means of an amplifier and conductors, any heat impulse of an object within it's range, is recorded in my laboratory, where it is again amplified and relayed to the alarm system. The most important feature of the system, is however, an ultra-high-frequency wave detector (also a Tesla invention), which is maintained in a poise in relation to normal surroundings, this also by means of a system of relays and amplifiers - sounds and records an alarm, if anything comes within it's range.

"Therefore in the early hours of last Tuesday morning, my alarm sounded, (and under normal conditions I would have awakened, but I was in profound sleep, induced by over-work) and I became aware of some disturbance only by degrees, and when I actually woke the alarm was not sounding, but heard the strange sound which I thought came from the Radio, but after a careful inspection of my alarm system, I found it had been in operation between two and two-thirty, and the reason I did not hear the alarm was an important part was fused, as if by a powerful current, evidence of some strange force on the mystery craft. This could be a new development of a foreign country or something from outer space! If this can be used beyond the range of our weapons, it would place us at the mercy of any country who had it, a small force in a space flyer would make armed resistance futile.

"Perhaps the oldest known records of space ships is found in the Hindu Classics Hamayana and Maha Bharata of Ancient India, while the Annals of Thutmose III of Ancient Egypt (1504-1450 B.C.) which are in the Vatican, give many stories of "Fire-Circles." There is also a space ship mentioned in Henry VI, Part 3, Act 2, Scene 1, by Shakespeare, and if one has the time to look through many other old dusty books, no doubt many other stories will be found.

"The Bible is full of such accounts. It is well worth ones time to search through the Bible books; I will list a few which I found very interesting. You might have to study the stories before you can get the correct picture. Not is it an interesting game, but it will give one a new, and perhaps a better, understanding of scripture. I hope so at any rate, so good hunting to you all.

"I found these: Genesis 18: verses 1 to 3; Genesis 19: 24-26; Exodus 3: 2-5; Exodus 13: 21-22; Exodus 14: 24; Exodus 19: 9-16 and 20; Exodus 34: 5-6. Judges 13: 3 & 24; II Kings 2: 1, 9, 10, 11; II Kings 6: 17; Psalms 60: 12; Psalms 68: 33, 34; Psalms 99: 7. Zechariah 5: 2; Isaiah 9: 8; Isaiah 16: 15; Isaiah 60: 8; Ezekiel 1: 4; Ezekiel 4: 22, 23; Ezekiel 10: all chapter. Dan 9; 21; Matthew 11: 9, 10; Matthew 25: 13; Mark 13: 27; Luke 21: 27; Acts 1: 9 to 11; Revelation 1: 7; Revelation 14: 6; Revelation 19: 17."

Chapter 15

Some remarks from the book "Return of the Dove" by Margaret Storm and Arthur Matthews.

God said, "Let there be light," so He made Tesla, and there was light!

-----

Today there are many "Space Ships" flying about everywhere,--their brilliant colours flashing like a peacock's tail, many of them come to us over great cosmic lightways, winging their way even without wings, travelling about God's great playground, propelled by the sustaining breath of His love for His children--even the foolish ones who now need be foolish no longer, for that is what makes it a time here on the planet Earth. We need be foolish no longer! Now we can awaken, stretch our minds and hearts up, up, up, until we hit a star. We have been prodigals for the last millions of years and the diet of husks has been awful. But the bad dream is over. We can relax and prepare for the feast--a grand and wonderful festival of human victory which will last for two thousand years. By that time we will have long since forgotten about the husks and the past years of planetary isolation, and we will be out there riding the lightways in space-ships, hopping from star to star on our cosmic assignment, while the great symphony of the spheres plays on and on and the angels sing! Of course, we still have with us in these latter days, the diehards, the spoil sports, the screw balls, the odd balls, the sad sacks, and a whole assortment of wet blankets in a wide variety of sizes, shapes, and shades. They are the ones with the souped-up egos. They do not buy the idea of space-ships, music of the spheres or the singing angels. They are the foolish ones who want to continue their foolishness.

In the hospital world that we have known for millions of years during our cosmic quarantine, it is correct to say that most of us have been foolish in the majority of our embodiments. We have been dreadful phonies, strictly hams, acting out roles on a stage called the world, a stage like a mixed-up, upside-down cake, with an animated crazy quilt for a platter, with such a design for living, it is a matter of no wonderment that whoever-is-in-charge had to send flying saucers to rescue us, warn, cajole or to just haul some of us off to a new dumping ground, to a new sort of hospital planet devoted exclusively to drying out wet blankets and removing the sadness from sacks -- and that, if you please, just at the moment when the chemise became high fashion. But those of us who are left here on the planet earth, who will continue our living here after the saucers have flown the cracked cups away to a new repair shop, -- well, we will have a whale of a clean-up job ahead of us because this globe has been lacking in good housekeeping for a long, long time. We will have to step out and keep up with the Joneses, only this time they don't live down the street; they live up there on those gay sparkling spheres called Venus, Mars, Jupiter, and so forth; and in places which sound like a melody -- Aquaria, Clarion, and a tiny little lighted jewel of a planet called Excelsior, which is said to be a delightful little place inhabited by little people, but real little people, very beautiful little men and women of exquisite stature, TOWERING TWO OR perhaps EVEN THREE INCHES IN HEIGHT.

They have perfect forms which move and float in rhythmic dances of breath-taking beauty and grace.  They have never known distress of any kind.  They are God's dedicated children.  Their Fire Dances in honour of the Sacred Flame, are all expressions of thanksgiving to their Creator for His gift of life.  That is their way of praying.  Dancing is to them synonomous with living, or the expressing of gratitude for the limitless cosmic abundance.  They are extremely artistic, and when they are not dancing, they are constantly helping the little nature spirits -- the fairies, the elves, the water sprites, -- to rearrange the decorations on the surface of their planet.  Perhaps a miniature rose tree just there, and a tiny waterfall plunging dizzily down from a sheer drop of six feet, would be effective as a backdrop for a new dance.  Are ideas such as these pondered by the little men and women who live on Excelsior?  The heavy foot of an earthling may never tread on Excelsior soil, but it is said that spaceships are equipped with marvelous viewing devices which will bring a planetary surface into a clear focus such as would make all Hollywood's cameras and screens seem like instruments as primitive as a stone arrowhead.  Truly, the cosmos is a place fascinating beyond the imagination of men, and best of all, it is man's heritage.  That is where we belong -- out there in the playground of the gods -- far beyond the silly sputniks, the false moons, the grapefruit sized satellites; even beyond the moon itself, and beyond the neighboring planets and stars and into THE great golden pathway of the Milky Way.  We belong far beyond all the rubbish and rubble of this once magnificent planet which we ourselves have turned into a hell.  The universe is our heritage and we have but to claim it, to explore it, to revel in its fathomless beauty.  It is all ours to use, to improve, and to love.  That is the clue.  It is ours to love.

But we have forgotten how to love natural things, -- God created things.  We love only our own grotesque miscreations; our mighty death-dealing weapons, our sculptured monuments marking blood-stained battlefields, our martial music designed to stir the hearts of men as they march forth to kill and to be killed, our guided missiles conceived by unguided men, left helpless and bereft without knowledge of their Sources; our ungreat bombs that can pulverize a great city at one blow.  We love to visit our spacious cemeteries, crowded to overflowing with the silent dead.  We love to bedeck the graves with ugly arrangements of withering flowers, piling death upon death.  We are sorry we could not give our beloved a more handsome tombstone, but taxes ride beside death on this planet.  You know how it is.  There was the hospital bill, the doctor's bill, the X-ray bill, the bill at the corner drugstore, plus a whopping big bill from the surgeon who cut and carved and sliced and sawed with all his might and main, while death just stood there and waited patiently.  It was by no whim of chance that our cosmic Hierarchy designated the earth as Planet "D" in this solar system.  That letter has come to stand for death, destruction, devastation, desperation, deficits, depletion, depression, devils and the DEW line.  It also stands for dainty dancers who have never known distress, but that is on the planet Excelsior.

Somewhere out there in space, somewhere out there where the wind is singing, where the air is fresh and sweet as white daisies laughing in the sun, the little planet spins on its course.  A tiny crystal globe is alight with the Sacred Flame, and around it the little men and women circle in their rhythmic dance, their hearts aflame with love of the One.  The little waterfall splashes merrily, a brilliant butterfly flits about the miniature rose tree and finds a resting place.  The stillness vibrates with rapture.  The dance goes on and on -- on Excelsior.  And here on Earth, death still rides in the saddle, but not for long.

Now in this glad November we can live with joy again. Now is the moment of appraisal. Now is the time to catch, to hold, to examine a fleeting cosmic instant covering nineteen million years in the cycle of human history on this planet earth. For now in these early November days of 1957, we know that the long and terrible chapter of human struggle has been finished. That is, it is finished for those who want it that way. For the others, -- the diehard skeptics, the sinister secretives, the know-it-alls, the so-whaters, -- for all these and others of their tribe, special provisions will be made, but elsewhere, SOMEWHERE, not here, not on this planet. For this planet has really had it, and far, far beyond the call of duty. That call first came sounding through the entire galaxy nineteen million years ago.

The universe had assembled a large number of refugees from other planets. These were the laggards, the leftovers, the rejected ones from those planets and stars in this and other solar systems. Using their free will in a destructive manner, they had made orphans of themselves by refusing the guidance of their own higher natures, their own Divine guided selves, and preferred to dally away their time in experimenting with miscreations of their own rather than in learning to create according to the Divine Plan. They contributed nothing constructive to the whole of which they were an integral part. They had skipped so many classes in learning, that they could not hope to catch up. Their miscreations proved so imperfect and destructive that they were finally refused further opportunities to incarnate within their own groups.

So the earth people came forward and offered to help the laggards by receiving them into families here. No other planet had a classroom for these problem students, or at least no other planet was willing to tackle the job of trying to redeem them. But the earth was a young planet, vigorous and strong, magnificently beautiful, abundant and full of promise. Disease was unknown. There was no distress in the sense of strain or pain. Members of the first root race were brought to the earth in a natural spaceship, a thought-controlled globe. They were accompanied by their teachers, sages and hierarchs representing the great cosmic Ray --.

This first group settled down in what is now familiarly known as the Grand Teton area in Wyoming. That country is still beautiful today, but in those days the entire globe was a sphere of unrivalled beauty. It is said that Amaryllis, the Godess of Spring, so loved the earth that she spent nine hundred years supervising its decoration, preparing it for the first guests. Over the entire globe the climate was always pleasant, neither too warm nor too cold, a land of eternal spring. There were no storms, floods, hurricanes, blizzards or natural catastrophes because there was no discord among the people.

Human beings definitely make their own troubles by their refusal to live as God intended them to live. Moreover, the clear and beautiful lower atmosphere around the earth became steadily more and more radiant as the Hierarches and sages instructed the people how to draw forth the goodness of the cosmic rays, to be used for any practical purpose that might arise. The earth people, living in this radiant atmosphere, were constantly bathed in these glorious emanations which flooded the earth from outer space, and then ascended back to the Source, for it is in the nature of the Flame, even physical fire, to rise. As a result the people felt bouyant, energized and spiritually attuned at all times. Their vision was unclouded and they had not only the visible and tangible evidence of the incoming Rays and the rising Flame, but they were in constant association with cosmic beings.

At the close of initiation into self-mastery, each individual then accomplished complete command over matter so that he was able to raise the vibration of the physical atoms which composed his body and ascend to his home star to await his next assignment.

Save for the long drag of time, the initiatory system on this planet remains the same today. At some time, in some embodiment, each individual must make his own Ascension. He must be able to achieve mastery over matter, raise the vibrations of his physical body, form a force field or personal spaceship and ascend to his home star.

During the present Aquarian Age all death, as we know it today, will cease on this planet. Each individual will be scientifically trained to make his Ascension, exactly as it is done on other planets.

The high hopes which the earth people had for the future, did not manifest. The laggards refused to comply with God's law. They insisted on using their own free will to create their own monstrous follies; they declined to assist in unfolding the Divine Plan. Moreover, they polluted and poisoned the radiant atmosphere with their astral emanations. Scorning all cooperative endeavors spiritually, they grew and matured in physical grossness; they mated and produced offspring of their kind; they poisoned their physical bodies with their own misguided emotions and thoughts of hatred; they introduced disease on the planet. They simply refused to believe in the one God.

The frightful contamination became worse; the atmosphere around the earth became gloomy and dark; the Cosmic Rays could no longer penetrate to the vegetation and soil. Only the physical sunlight devoid of the life-giving God-essence of the great universal Virtues, reached the people. No longer did the earth give forth its natural note of harmony; its great vibrant chords were missing from THE MUSIC OF THE SPHERES. No longer did the earth give off light, for the Flame had ceased to rise. This in brief, is the story of the fall of man.

Man became wise in his own foolish self-esteem. Conditions became so hopeless that God decided to destroy the world. The Scriptures carry the account of this great deluge, together with the significant statement that the world would again be destroyed, but by fire from heaven rather than water. History of humanity appears to be in its Fifth Root Race and now is the time when the final cleansing is to take place on the earth's surface, within the interior of the planet which had also become contaminated and in the astral atmosphere of the earth, which now extends 10,000 feet above the surface of the globe. It is in this astral area around the earth that all of the contamination has accumulated from the emotional emanations given off by individuals through the ages, and where hover the frightful thought-forms thrown off by the race. The contaminated astral atmosphere around the earth although still being constantly poisoned by emanations of hatred vengeance, greed and lust generated by living human beings, is being bombarded night and day by powerful rays directed from spaceships orbiting the earth, by cleansing energies from saucers flying close to the earth. Although disease and death, and all the old fears of poverty, war, hunger, and helplessness still stalk the earth, these grim spectors are attracted hence only by the unlighted ones, by the diehards, the sinister secretives, the stubborn skeptics. In other words by the laggards who are still lagging.

But material situations will be so greatly improved within a few years that the planet will be unrecognizable according to present low standards. The globe, during the past, became so heavily weighted with discord that it drooped on its bent axis like a weary flower on a stalk. Now the supreme power is straightening the axis. Meanwhile, the earth is moving in a sidewise motion as it edges into a new orbit, and, at the same time, is being lifted up spiralling into a new spacial region. In the near future, the natural action of the cosmic rays will bring about a complete restoration of the planet. It will again become a paradise as it was before God made man. What we know as the astral atmosphere will be completely dispelled. Light from the cosmic rays will reach the earth in natural abundance. The climate will change so that the spring-like weather will take charge all year round. With the incoming light, the atmosphere of the earth will again become brilliant with colours; the sphere will sound forth its great chords in the cosmic symphony. Disease will vanish and its memory will be wiped from the minds of men.

All of this is in the future when the words of the Lord's prayer shall become manifest --- "Thy kingdom come, Thy Will be done, on earth as it is in Heaven." If there is to be heaven on this earth then it is natural to assume that there will be no place on this planet for the obstructionists, the unlighted ones who are haunted by doubt, fear, hate and greed.

This book is therefore of interest only to those who know in their hearts that they truly desire to serve the Light. That, as such servers, they really wish to take part in the unfoldment of the Divine Plan on this planet. We need not waste time and energy trying to convince the unlighted ones that God is a good God. If they have not figured that out in the past, it is hardly likely that they will learn to lovingly entertain the idea during the future.

Therefore, only those who are interested in taking part in ushering in the new civilization should read this book. Among those bent on vengeance, war, financial profit, and so forth, this book will only arouse further antagonism and jealousy. Where their future lies is a matter of no interest to us, whatsoever. Those who are not with God are against Him and that settles the matter.

Our entire energy now must be thrown on the positive side. We must study the situation as of today, find out just where we stand, discover what progress has been made, and what remains to be done. How can we help? What positive enterprises, no matter how tiny or how great, can we initiate?

Even now, like Noah of old, we gaze expectantly skyward, knowing that the Dove is winging its way from outer space, bearing to us the symbolic olive branch from our planetary neighbours, those good friends we knew and loved so well. They are coming again. Now let us prepare for the great reunion of fellowship, of interplanetary friendship. Let us prepare to welcome the Dove and send forth to all mankind the joyous message of good will to all.

# Chapter 16

The earth is being drenched with the cosmic ray, coming in from outer space, and focused upon this planet by beamed direction from certain other planets and stars, which serve as great reservoirs for this cosmic energy. At the very center of the earth certain rays carrying certain colours meet, forming the polarities and axis; this central orb or kingdom formed by the rays is under Divine Law. In this central orb, the rays and colours are blended, and now, they constantly surge up and through the earth, washing over every single atom that makes up the globe, including mankind.

In olden times, the earth was known to be one of God's many mansions, as are all planets and stars. The center of the earth was regarded as the central alter of the planet, upon which eternally blazed the sacred Flame. The light from this reflected to and through every atom. Perhaps in time, this reflection will cleanse the soil of all strontium poisoning resulting from nuclear test fallouts. The strontium was released by stupid and misguided men, dedicated to deeds of voilence. The tests are still blasting away, making more work for the cosmic ray.

Mankind does these foolish things. Instead of considering the One God, we find men and women everywhere, running helplessly and hopelessly in pursuit of the many things which they think will increase their happiness. Yet they wonder why they continue to suffer. Mistake on top of mistake. They never appear to learn. They wonder why they must endure a twilight existence only to face death as a finality. The answer is that they judge by appearances. Because the majority of people are troubled, they rashly assume that trouble is inevitable. Because the majority of people die, they rashly assume that death is a normal and natural change. Because the majority of people are often angry, hostile, aggravated people, full of hate and misery, this condition is accepted as the rule for all mankind on this earth. It is, they say, the way the ball bounces.

But during the next two thousand years, all these delusions will be dispelled. As soon as the people from other planets are received in friendship, we will quickly realize that we, as earth people, and as very, very stupid people, are much in the minority in this solar system. We will quickly realize that trouble is not a natural or normal condition for us. Trouble is an atheistic condition, brought on by the earth people who have lost contact with their Maker, lost faith in Him, and therefore have lost all knowledge of how to live as we should. Without God in our hearts, we poison the soil, the atmosphere and our own bodies with hate, openly inviting disease, disaster and death.

If, as we pretend to believe, God is good and perfect, and man is made in His image and likeness even to being endowed with a free will, then why should imperfection be accepted? We were told to be perfect, even as our Father in Heaven is perfect. We should busy ourselves calling forth perfection, impressing it upon suffering matter, so that the matter can send forth the radiant energy of love rather than a vibration of pain. Man has misused his free will, has misspent his God-given energy, and has filled the earth with monstrous miscreations entirely of his own making. Because he has been willing to accept imperfection, he has not asked for help from his ever-present Maker, but has gone ahead on his own, trying constantly to improve his lot by exchanging one imperfection for another which he hopes will prove slightly less imperfect.

Man has attempted to build entire complex civilizations by using judgement based on appearances. Now science comes forward, following the power-crazed war machine in a frenzied pace to keep us with things as they appear to be. Or as the misguided scientists and politicians think things ought to be. The be-wildered public is told that this is progress. Exactly since when, has progress been based on fear, the one and only weapon available to the dark forces? So while the dark forces entrenched in science are busy creating imperfect systems to bolster up already imperfect systems, our hearts need not be troubled. We can turn abruptly from this negative point of view and look upon the positive surge toward perfection which is now rapidly engulfing the human family. We can happily see now how the whole world of appearances will vanish within the transmuting power of the cosmic ray, which is now almost upon us.

It might appear that little has been accomplished during the past two thousand years, but remember what Jesus said. "Let not your heart be troubled." The most outstanding opportunity before us now lies in our acceptance of the hand of friendship extended to us by our neighbours from other lands and other planets in our solar system. The great message of truth that the Venusians and others wish to convey to us today is identical with the universal truth established by Jesus. As soon as interplanetary communication is established on a world-wide scale, the earth people will quickly realize that they have been foolish to have wasted their time and money, listening to so-called authorities, who have sold their lies at a high price.

The truth has always been free. No one can purchase it, for it only comes directly from the One God through His One Divine Son Jesus. This has been the message from Venus, from the first visit. They are still sending the same old (but very new) message. The good news which Christ tried to teach us, sets us free. What is this freedom? Freedom for man comes to him as a result of his using God-free energy in its natural free way. God-energy in its pure form flows into man heartbeat by heartbeat. As the pure electrons are released by the sacred three-fold Flame within the heart, they enter the bloodstream. As they enter they are immediately qualified or stamped with the pattern of the individual. They can be qualified with love or they can be misqualified with hate. In other words the electrons, which provide all power, can be used to carry out loving deeds, to think loving thoughts, to speak loving words - or they can be used in an opposite manner, depending upon the choice we make through the use of our free will. When man misuses this electronic power in performing hateful acts, he misqualifies the energy. In other words he leaves his stamp of imperfection upon millions of electrons that flow into his blood-stream. This energy is God-energy and as such it must obey the free will of man, for man is the reflection of God, created as a free being. When man chooses to enslave this free and pure energy, so that it will do his bidding and supply him with power to carry out some questionable enterprise, he thereby enslaves himself. He starts each pure electron on its way through hiw own bloodstream with a handicap - the weight of his own feeling of discord.

The electron itself remains pure, for it is God-energy and can know no impurity. But as it whirls on its course, it collects around itself a shell of impure matter; the same murky gray astral matter that the laggards brought to earth. As it takes its appointed place with other electrons and forms an atom, the sticky substance clings, and soon the revolution of the electrons within the atom is slowed by clogging. Then the revolution of the atom itself is slowed, and in addition, the atom collects the same astral substance on its outer shell, adding further weight.

The resulting rate of electronic revolutions, plus atomic revolutions, taken as a whole in a man's physical, etheric, emotional and mental bodies, constitute what is known as his state of consciousness or his vibratory note. If his electrons and atoms are revolving slowly, he is not only subject to disease, but he is subject to ugly delusions such as death. He begins to feel old age creeping on and in his limited understanding, he assumes that death is not far away. He feels fearful, bereft and alone. He cannot understand who he is or why he is here; he has no purpose in accord with the Divine Plan. He is, in short, a materialist, weighted down by his own burdens of hate which he carries right within his own atoms. He tends to be separative in relation to his God and his fellow men because he is usually quite charmed by the amount of astral debris he has accumulated in his atomic structure. The weight of the misqualified energy he is using, places him under the delusion that the rioting forces within gives him power. He throws his weight around, as the popular saying goes. He likes to give orders, put people in their places, clamp down on this situation or that, and in general act like a big shot.

If he happens to be a scientist seeking to ferret out the secrets of atomic power, he can only react according to the limitations he has imposed upon his own atomic structure. He therefore, seeks to enslave the atom, just as he has enslaved his own atoms that he lives with each day. He can think of atomic power only in the terms of fission and fusion. He wants to split the atom, to tear it apart by brute force, to strip it bare as one would strip the skin off an orange. His way is the way of fear, of hate, of snickering smugness.

The individual who is not separated from his God by this barrier of astral debris within his body, seeks to become a co-worker, to serve his God. He daily works with the Rays and the Flames, which are only other names for the Christ-Truth. He forms a close friendship with the One whom he can trust, One who built this planet, with his Father. Knowing this truth, we become completely free. Our free minds then clearly see the glad reason for all this, and we then understand the cosmic ray. How different is the way of Jesus compared with the way of the fission-fusion scientists, for the way of Jesus is love.

Yes, the true program for the Aquarian Age is the way of Christ Jesus, for true Love is the greatest power, the only power, which will or can defeat the atomic bomb.

In the following chapters are set forth the broad outlines of the "New Age" program as it has manifested in recent years, and as it will affect the immediate future of every earth person, indeed of every earth atom. Since the program is in the final analysis, a scientific one, designed to prepare individuals for the future life, we will focus our attention first upon the vast preparatory work which was started in 1856 by that great scientific genius, Nikola Tesla.

According to the world at large, Tesla had strange ideas. He always thought he came from the planet Venus. He said as much to me, and the crew of a Venus spaceship said in one of their first messages, that a male child was 'born' on board their ship during its trip from Venus to Earth in July, 1856. The little boy was called Nikola (which is the name of his family town, in reverse, on Venus. That is the town of ALOKIN. The ship landed at midnight, between July ninth and tenth, in a remote mountain province in what is now Yugoslavia. There, according to arrangements, the child was placed in the care of a good man and his wife. This message was first received by Arthur Matthews of Lake Beauport, Quebec, Canada, an electrical engineer who from boyhood was closely associated with Tesla.

In 1944, a year after the death of Tesla, the late John J. O'Neill, then science editor of the New York Herald Tribune, wrote an excellent story of Tesla's life and work, entitled "Prodigal Genius." O'Neill made the common error of assuming that Tesla had died and left no disciples. O'Neill could not have been more mistaken. In the first place Tesla was not a mortal according to earth standards. His thinking and his work was several hundred years ahead of earth standards. Years before he died, he entrusted Arthur Matthews, of Canada, with many tasks which are of vital current interest. To name tow -- the Tesla interplanetary communication system and the anti-war machine. Mr. Matthews built a model Tesla set which is named "The Tesla Scope" in 1938. This was designed after the first model which Tesla built, with Matthews in 1917, during the First World War. This is a very simple machine, operated by the use of cosmic rays. Other models were built by Matthews in 1948, and a more recent model in 1967. The original design was given to Matthews by Tesla, and experiments were made with this receiver by Tesla with the help of Matthews, during the first world war. That is between 1917 and 1920. There were experiments also, with what is now known as radar, on the beach at Tadoussac, between that small town and along the beach to Riviere Portneuf. Both towns are on the north side of the great St. Lawrence River. At this spot the river is about twenty-two miles wide, from North to South. Experiments were also made between both sides of the river with radar and the special receiver. After experimenting at this place, work was extended to Lake St. John at a private camp, located near Lake Edward, owned at that time by Major Henry Sanford, of New York City. (A personal friend of Tesla and Matthews).

A complete electrical laboratory was built at Sanford by the Major, and in this well-equipped shop was first developed radar and micro-waves. A third model of the Tesla Scope was also built here. During this time, between the years 1922 until 1930, we were able to keep in touch with Tesla at New York, by means of direct contact with micro waves. (Waves of less than one degree). The complete transmitter was built into a case only 3" x 2" x 2". This was battery operated, using the Tesla mercury cell, and was a complete telephone, something much like the modern walkie-talkie.

Some years after the above experiments, Arthur Matthews obtained the old farm at Lake Beauport. It was on this spot that the first practical radar was developed and built, from the working knowledge obtained from our experiment at Tadoussac. A number of other ideas of Tesla were also developed. One of these was a large air-core transformer. The very high voltage developed by this was used for a guide station. It generated a 'standing beam' which Tesla said extended directly upwards for a distance of about 30,000 miles. (It was thus used as a guide for the spacecraft which Tesla expected would land on my property, some time). It was due to this marker that the Venus ship has always landed at the exact same position. Not by a lucky chance, but pure design.

Now before we go further into that, let us review a bit about the early life of Tesla, and by doing so try to clear up many mistakes some writers have made. The following is from the words of Tesla himself as told to Arthur Matthews between the years 1917 and 1943. Much of this was recorded on the Tesla high-frequency voice recorder. This is something like the well known tape recorder, but it does not use any form of tape or wire, nor does it have any moving parts.

Historians agree that Nikola Tesla was born at midnight, between July 9th and 10th, in the year 1856. Djouka Tesla, the mother was a most remarkable woman and assuredly possessed advanced spiritual powers. She was the eldest child in a family of seven children. (Lucky number 7). Her father was a minister of the Serbian Orthodox Church. Her mother became blind after the seventh child was born, and Djouka unhesitatingly took charge of the entire household. She never attended school, nor did she learn even the rudiments of reading and writing, at home. Yet she moved with ease in cultured circles as did her family. Here was a woman who could neither read nor write, yet she possessed literary abilities far beyond those of a person of considerable education. Tesla himself, never wearied of talking about his remarkable mother, and described how she had absorbed "by ear" all the cultural riches of her community and her nation. Like Nikola, she apparently had the power of instant recall. Nikola said that she could easily repeat thousands of verses of the national poetry of her country. It was because of her great interest in poetry that Nikola, in his busy American days as a super-man, still found time to translate and have published some of the best examples of Serbian sagas.

His mother was also famed throughout her home provinces for her artistic ability, often expressed in beautiful needlework. She possessed remarkable manual desterity and Nikola said her fingers were so sensitive that she could tie three knots in an eyelash, even when she was past sixty years of age. She had an excellent grasp of philosophy and apparently a practical understanding of mechanical and technical devices. She needed a loom for household weaving, so she designed and built one. She did not think of herself as an inventor, yet she built many labor-saving devices and instruments for her household. In addition she was so skillful in handling business and financial matters that she managed all accounts for her household as well as for her husband's church.

Nikola's father was the son of an army officer, and as a young man set out on a military career. But he was soon disillusioned for he was irked by the discipline, and turned to his true calling in the literary field. He wrote poetry, articles on current problems, and philosophical essays. This led quite naturally, to the ministry, giving him an opportunity to write sermons and to speak from the pulpit. He did not limit himself to the usual church topics, but ranged far and wide, covering subjects of local and national interest concerning labour, social and economic problems. Until Nikola was seven years of age, the father had a parish church at Smilijan, an agricultural community in a high plateau region in that part of the Alps which stretch from Switzerland to Greece.

This then was the childhood environment of the boy from Venus. It was a life filled with joy. He had an ideal home with a loving, understanding family. He lived in a magnificent countryside, close to nature. He was a boy like other little boys up to a certain point; the point at which he became the superboy, foreshadowing the superman. And so it was that he lacked human companions, a state, not of loneliness, but of aloneness that was to continue for a long time. He chose his friends with a wisdom we see in few humans. He had the deep-set piercing eyes of the thinker. Deep blue in colour, they were honest, kind eyes, for he was an honest man, and whatever you are shows in your eyes, for they are the reflection of your soul.

In my story, I will only state that which I know and try to enlighten those who have perhaps been deceived by reading untrue stories about Tesla.

The powers possessed by him were in no sense psychic powers. The ability to visualize unthought of things, - new things - and mold them into something real, such as the motors, and other wonderful things, as did Tesla, has nothing to do with the astral plane. For when Tesla wanted something, he went straight to God. Nothing complicated about his approach for God is the only author of science and invention. The ability to visualize comes from training. Any one, without any formal education, can talk to God, but it needs a bit of something

113

more TO LISTEN WHEN GOD SPEAKS. A person who knows and loves God possesses powers which enable him to stand on this earth and yet observe incidents on Venus, Mars or the Moon. He can also look out over the earth and sweep the entire scene with one glance. He can look through the earth and watch activities within the dense physical globe. Thus it will be realized that the person who truly loves God, is completely free. He can see above, as below.

The person with astral vision is a prisoner of his own limited and highly questionable power. Peace of mind and serenity of soul do not lie along that route, nor can the Voice of the Silence be heard within the beating heart of the unlighted ones who amuse themselves with such nonsense. Astral vision is more often a sign of regression than advancement, for it simply denotes the attainment of certain animal characteristics. It must be remembered that all animals in certain advanced groups; dogs, cats, horses and elephants, have astral vision. Many other animals also possess it and most animals are telepathic within certain limits.

In humans, this type of clairvoyance is often associated with solar plexus telepathy, another animal characteristic. Many persons who use solar plexus telepathy are inclined to confuse it with mental telepathy, and those who practice mental telepathy are frequently unaware that the only type of telepathy which can be considered as spiritual power is from soul to soul. That is two persons completely in tune with each other, or in tune with Divine Will, or Spirit.

Individuals who strive to cultivate their astral abilities, even though they may be born with them, are following an extremely dangerous course. One which can easily lead from psychism to black magic and from black magic to insanity. If an individual is born with psychic powers he should either banish them at all costs, or take up the proper study which will enable him to serve God to the limit of his capability. These are thoughts which if properly channelled can lead to discipleship, but if not properly channelled, they can and will lead to mediumship and misery. Mediumship is the way of retrogression; discipleship is the way to the path of truth, light, beauty, and unlimited cosmic freedom.

Every individual has only one rule to follow and this is it: "Place yourself at all times under the full power and protection of Divine Mind."

There is no need to be running around the world searching for a Guru or Master. When you are ready to be of service to your Maker, He will seek you.

Tesla discovered this truth at an early age. His study of the Bible enabled him to conceive 1,200 inventions, and so the part he was to play in the Divine Plan unfolded quickly. He enrolled at the Gymnasium at Gospic, a town to which his father had been assigned as a minister. Here Tesla discovered that his favourite subjects were the Bible and mathematics. In the school at Gospic, Nikola first came to desire to retain his ability to visualize real things, which could be used then, and in the future. From the study of such an old book as the Bible, which had been written thousands of years before he was born, he desired to bring this gift under full control and use it, as a tool, rather than allow it to use him.

Nikola had no wish to be submerged in paper work, even in his school days, a thought which might be of value to many business and government executives today. Nikola found that he did not need to go to the blackboard in the classroom to work out a problem. At the thought of a blackboard, it would appear in the ether before him.  As the problem was stated it appeared instantly on the etheric blackboard, together with all the symbols and operations required to work out the solution.  Each step appeared instantly and much more rapidly than anyone could possibly work out the problem on paper or slate.  Therefore by the time the whole problem had been stated, Nikola could give the solution immediately.

At first his teachers thought he was just an extremely clever boy who had found some method of cheating.  However, in a short time they were forced to admit that no deception could possibly be practiced, so they gladly accepted the glamour shed abroad as the rumour got around that the Gospic classroom was graced by a genius.  Nikola never bothered to explain about the etheric blackboard for he intuitively knew he would not be believed.

Always through the passing years, he guarded his power as the great spiritual treasure he knew it to be.  He used the same power to replace all customary memory functions, and soon he discovered that he could learn foreign languages with little of the usual effort.  He became proficient in German, French, and Italian in those early years, and this opened up to him entire new worlds that remained closed to other students.  His father's library contained hundreds of fine books and by the time Nikola was eleven years old, he had read them all.

He had little in common with his school mates, and, in fact little in common with his teachers.  But they accepted him because he was a lovable lad without a trace of arrogance or pride.  Neither did he surround himself in an exaggerated sense of humility.  He was a normal, natural, friendly boy living in a natural, friendly world.  On fine summer days, he would often wander over the mountains to sit again beside the brook at Smilijin, and watch his little waterwheel in operation; the wheel he had designed and installed.

He was constantly working on mechanical devices during the year he was in school at Gospic, but the school offered no courses that could help him; not even a course in manual training.  In his home hung a picture which he had often carefully studied.  His Uncle explained that it was a picture of Niagara Falls in America.  Filled with prophetic joy he exultantly turned to his Uncle and said, "Some day I am going to America and harness Niagara Falls for power."

Thirty years later, he carried out his plan, exactly as he had predicted it at the age of ten years.

# Chapter 17

In the book, "Return of the Dove" by Margaret Storm, mention is made of the "wall of light." Many mistaken ideas have come from that story.

It was Tesla who conceived the idea of the wall of light during his early life. Very few earth people have been able to build this wall of light, because, in the first place, they have received the wrong instructions.

Exactly what is this wall of light? How can it be built? Who can build it? What will it accomplish? The great mistake some persons have made, from reading "Return of the Dove" is the idea that it is man-made. This is not so. The protective wall of light is the power of God. It has nothing to do with will power. The wall cannot be "built" or "formed" around a person or persons. The fact is, this wall, (or tube as some say) is already built. It is all around us. It fills all space, and it has only to be accepted as a gift, and used. Its use depends on perfect faith in the ability, and the wish of God to protect all those who call upon Him.

Tesla believed in this Divine Power. This is what he termed the "WALL OF LIGHT." The thought power which operates the Venus spaceship is no more or less than the perfect faith which Christ said would move mountains. From his Bible study Tesla knew and believed in this great power, which is free for any person to use. It only comes to those who accept Jesus Christ as the only Son of the living God. No doubt the actual reasons why Tesla's scientific methods are not taught in our school system is the fact he brings God into the picture. The colleges cannot find professors who understand real science, the Bible or Tesla, for no one can understand true science or Tesla, unless he is in tune with the Divine Spirit. Why not train teachers? One reason might be that the adoptions of Tesla's inventions and his faith in the power of God, will disturb the status quo. They will offer a whole new way of life, they will upset churchianity, they will make the establishment of world-wide free Christianity possible and desirable. They will cast profitmaking high rates of interest and political conniving into oblivion and will make the present economic system look exactly like the silly thing it is.

Tesla was always a happy man, and the stories told about his last years are not true. He was never in need and died a rich man. He received an income very much larger than the amount which some reports say he received. He was never in debt and as a Christian he died a happy man.

On an October night in 1956, when a group of friends met in New York City to talk of U.F.O., very little was known by any of them about Tesla or his work. Over in Paris a Spacecraft convention was held for interested Europeans. Arther H. Matthews of Lake Beauport, Quebec, Canada, submitted a paper on the Tesla set for interplanetary communication, which he had built and was then operating. A report on this paper reached New York a few weeks later and contact with Mr. Matthews was established by correspondence. That was the start of the new interest in the work of Tesla. Imagine! He had worked most of his life in America, and few, if anyone remembered either him or his work.

Perhaps some one will ask, "What was Tesla's work?" Well, for one thing, he invented the 20th century. Almost everything which the world of today considers important, came from Tesla. The world of today and for the next five hundred years at least, will be the world of Tesla, for there are nearly 1,100 Tesla inventions not yet well known to the public. Imagine! A car operated without any fuel; your house lit and heated by the sun. Free. Yes, even when you do not see the sun. A voice and thought-operated recorder and typewriter. A two way portable telephone and T.V. which can operate over a distance of 8,000 miles, which in size can fit into your coat pocket and is operated by means of the Tesla battery which is kept charged by the sun. An aircraft which has no engine, no fuel, no wings and no noise, lands at a speed of less than one mile per hour.

These are just a few of the 1,100 inventions of Tesla, to say nothing about the 100 now in world-wide us, under different trade names, but which a look at the patents, will prove are Tesla's. T.V., radio, radar, all electric light and power, all auto controls which are used to make the moon rockets work, all those new power developments, transmission lines, the microwaves, even your modern car works because Tesla's spark coil makes it run. All these things just because a little boy loved God, and used his head and body to serve God, not as a garbage dump for drugs and smoke. Imagine what good could be done if more people used their bodies and minds as Tesla did.

Did you know that the tall towers used for T.V. and microwaves are not required if the Tesla system was completely adopted? All those poles we see in town and other places are not needed. The Tesla anti-war machine follows the same principle. It requires no poles, no lines or large reflectors mounted on towers. Neither does it require an army to maintain it. It does provide positive protection for any coast line or national border. It is not in any sense, a fence. The whole thing depends upon the "peaks" which are, of course, invisible to the human eye. All electric currents of whatever frequency pass in the earth and can be made to "peak" or bounce up above the earth at regular measured distances.

So far as the sputniks and other orbiting devices are concerned, these could not be designed to drop destruction on us from up above, if the Tesla anti-war machine was functioning. In addition to the protecting wall of power, the machine can also be built with a ceiling. If Tesla's machine is adopted there is nothing that can affect it; nothing in the way of an A bomb or H bomb or any other bomb, even if it is transported on a missle, rocket or a sutnik. In the first place and this is the important point, once Tesla's machine is set up, no form of bomb or high explosive can be made. In other words, if some nut tried to make a bomb and Tesla's machine was functioning, the bomb would explode right there, whether underground, in the air or any other place. So along with the adoption of the Tesla idea, no form of bomb or high explosive such as the A bomb or H bomb would continue to exist.

In a letter which Tesla wrote to me in 1935, he said, speaking of his anti-war machine: "My discovery ends the menace of airplanes, submarines, rock-ets or space machines, regardless of their height or speed. A century from now every nation will render itself immune from attack by my device."

I believe, as I believe in God, that the adoption of Tesla's machine will prevent war. Actually I have been fighting for Tesla to have the world give him credit for the many wonderful things he has done. I have written hundreds of letters, newspaper and magazine articles about his inventions, to help the world know more about this wonderful man.

Yes, indeed. The world should know more about Tesla, but the hundreds of letters received, clearly show that most people are just finding out how to spell his name. Almost every letter received begins something like this: "I never heard of Tesla until I read your excerpts from 'Return of the Dove.' Where can we find out more about this wonderful man?"

Well. No one will find out more about him, if the Silence group has its way. There is very little published about him, except, maybe, the copies of his patents, which can still be obtained from the patent office. I would suggest that if anyone is truly interested, they write to the patent office for a list and price of the Tesla inventions. Anyone who can read and who is sincerely interested in science,will find these patents highly interesting and instructive. Not every person will be able to understand them; they require most careful study.

Perhaps it will be interesting to give a short outline of Tesla's achievements. The field of invention has never known a genius as successful in developing far-reaching and original inventions, such as those of this great man, whose name should be known in every corner of the globe for his outstanding scientific achievements. Most writers state that Tesla was born in 1856 in Smilijan, Lika, border country of Austria-Hungary, but that is about all they do state. Little is said or known about his achievements.

Tesla's practical career started in 1881, in Budapest, Hungary, where he made his first electrical invention, a telephone repeater, and conceived the idea of the rotating magnetic field, which later made him world famous. It may not be amiss to devote a few moments here to the manner in which this prime of savants approached the idea of the rotating field and induction motor.

One day, while attending the University, one of the Professors was demonstrating an experiment with the Gramme armature type of dynamo, when the idea occurred to the young physicist that the sparking of the commutator, which he alone had minutely observed, could be eliminated. The professor immediately denied that this was possible, but with a steady mind and self-conviction, young Tesla determined to work out his ideas. The result was that the modern induction motor was developed, which operates solely from alternating current and requires no commutator of any kind, thus overcoming the nuisance of sparking inherent in former type direct-current machines. Realizing the value of his invention, he left for France in an effort to interest someone in his device, but his efforts proved fruitless. At the time he was employed by a prominent European engineering concern, but hearing of the rapid growth of the electrical industry in America, he promptly decided to come to that country, which he did in 1884 and since then, became a naturalized citizen of the United States.

To this country, he brought with him, the various models of the first induction motors, which were eventually shown to George Westinghouse, and it was in the Westinghouse shops that the induction motor was perfected by Nikola Tesla.

Numerous patents were taken out on this phenomenal prime-mover, all of which are under Tesla's name, and he was therefore the first person, beyond the shadow of a doubt, to introduce the rotating field principle, in perfecting the induction motor, which is today universally used. Large sums of money were expended by Tesla to protect his patents on this prime-mover, and he was at the time not permitted to express himself in print or give the history of his invention. Thus many erroneous impressions were entertained regarding his inventions.

Later, another type of machine was brought out by him, in connection with his work in electric power transmission. This one had a field energized by currents of different phase relation (i.e., while one current was at zero amplitude the other would be at maximum etc.) producing a rotating field in which conductors were employed, and in this way the high frequency current was obtained. This type of machine was subsequently developed to perfection and the principle is described in his patent, dated 1889. His next work which attracted universal attention was the production of high frequency currents at high potentials, tremendous electrical discharges. All of these experiments were first performed by this genius and never duplicated. One of the first high tension apparatus built by Tesla, was first used in Europe by Lord Kelvin, the noted English mathematician and scientist, who used it for his lecture demonstrations at the Royal Society.

Tesla's most important work at the end of the nineteenth century was his original system of transmission of energy by wireless. In 1900 Tesla obtained his two fundamental patents on the transmission of true wireless energy covering both methods and apparatus and involving the use of four tuned circuits. He also obtained a number of other patents at the same time, describing many other improvements. Among these may be mentioned his application of refrigeration and the oscilatory system with which he obtained remarkable results in his well equipped laboratory on Houston Street, New York City.

In 1901 and 1902 several patents were granted to him describing a number of improvements, among which, two assumed great importance in the radio art. One of these was known under the name of the 'tone wheel' and the other, the 'tikker.' Other persons claimed the inventions, but Tesla was the real inventor. At a little later date Tesla secured two patents on what he termed the principle of individualization, involving the use of more than one oscillation for the operation of receiver. This property is known under the name of beat receptors.

In long protracted interference proceedings carried on in 1903, however, Tesla was accorded full and undisputed priority over all other claimants. A patent was granted to Tesla in 1914 on an improvement of far-reaching importance in radio and T.V. work. The application was filed in 1902. It describes a new form of transmitter with which, according to Tesla's statement, an unlimited quantity of energy can be transmitted from a small and compact plant. This transmitter possesses the wonderful feature whereby static, the great nuisance of radio can be completely eliminated, because of the speed with which receivers can be operated; it being possible to throw them in and out of tune by a variation of not more than one thousandth of one per cent of the wave length. Tesla also evolved a static preventor which was successfully tested, and proved perfect.

This great scholar and philosopher did not devote his time to electrical devices alone, but turned his attention to many other fields. He developed a steam and gas turbine, which developed more power than any other motor or engine ever built. It developed 20 horse-power for each pound of engine weight. This turbine should be used in our present day automobiles, aeroplanes, and many other land and water vehicles.

This master magician, upon whose inventions this modern world depends for its existence, spent a fabulous amount of time and money in perfecting his inventions, which, as I have stated before, numbered 1,200 up to his death in 1943. Perhaps of the total, only a little over 100 are in everyday use, and most of them are not known under his name. Tesla invented the twentieth century. The general use of his other inventions will make another new world, and prevent all future wars, for his greatest invention (that of 1934) was conceived to prevent war.

This is the idea with which we first experimented at Lake Beauport, Quebec, Canada. It includes in its design that which is known today as radar, the idea which Tesla invented before the first world war.

It is interesting to know what Tesla thought concerning "Research." He made the following remarks in 1916, quoted from a letter received from Nikola Tesla to Arthur Matthews, July 9th, 1916.

"I have called it material research because I wanted to exclude immaterial research. I class under this head pure thought as distinct from thought mixed with matter. It is worth while making this distinction, for from the youngest to the oldest chemist, it is not always recognized. It is very natural for us to think we can think new things into being. Chemistry has advanced only in proportion to the handling of chemical substances by some one. When the study of our science was largely mental speculation, and the products and reagents largely immaterial, like fire and phlogiston, we advanced but slowly. Ages of immaterial research for the philosopher's stone only led to disappointment. Successful results in modern times came from following nature, learning by asking and experimenting; reasoning just enough from one stage of acquired knowledge to ask the next question of materials.

"In speaking of research, I do not mean to confine my thoughts to the chemists and their knowledge and literature, but rather to that science which is back of chemistry. We may call it natural science, if we are careful. It includes for my present purposes, all philosophy based on measurable facts. Psychology and therapeutics come under this head, so do electricity, anatomy and physics, chemistry and biology. These are inquisitive sciences, where the answers come from asking questions of nature. If I can leave with you even a faint impression of the importance of new knowledge, the strength to be gained from its acquirement, and the pleasure in the process itself, I shall feel repaid. So much useful pioneer work in all fields has been done with simple material equipment coupled with good mental equipment, that it almost seems as though this was the rule. The telegraph and telephone started with a few little pieces of wire wound by hand with paper insulation. The basic work on heredity was carried out by an Austrian monk with a few garden peas. The steam engine came from the kitchen fire. There was, however, the same general kind of mind behind each one of these discoveries, THE MIND OF THE TRAINED INQUIRER."

Most people have never heard of Tesla, yet he was the world's greatest inventor in all history. He obtained more revolutionary patents than anyone in history. Science accords to him over seventy-five original discoveries, not mere mechanical improvements. Tesla was an originator, a pioneer blazing the trail. Aside from this he was a discoverer of the highest order. When he died in 1943, he left the world richer by over a thousand inventions that God had allowed him to conceive. With his passing I lost a very old friend, and because of my intense admiration for him, I wrote "Tribute to Nikola Tesla" which was published by a number of newspapers, and which is included in this work as Chapter 12, Part II.

# Chapter 18

All electrical machinery using or generating alternating current is due to Tesla. High tension current transmission without which the modern world would be dead, is all due to the genius of Tesla. The world did not know of Tesla because he committed the unpardonable crime of not having a permanent press agent to shout his greatness from the housetops. Then too, most of his inventions, at least to the public mind, are more or less intangible on account of the fact that they are very technical and therefore do not catch the popular imagination. The trouble with Tesla was that he lived at least a century ahead of his time. He was often denounced as a dreamer even by well-informed men. He was called crazy by others who should have known better. For Tesla talked in a language that most people did not understand and still do not.

In 1893, three years before anyone else made any attempt to use wireless telegraphy (radio), Tesla first described his system and took out patents on a number of novel devices which were then but imperfectly understood. Even the electrical world at large laughed at these patents. But large wireless interests had to pay him tribute in the form of real money, because his "fool" patents were recognized to be fundamental. He actually antedated every important radio invention. Tesla was a man of extraordinary knowledge. He was remarkably well read and had a photographic memory whereby it was possible for him to recite page after page of nearly every classical work, -- be it Goethe, Voltaire, or Shakespeare. He spoke and wrote twleve languages. He was an accomplished calculator, who had little use for tables and text-books, and held the slide rule in contempt. Tesla received numerous honours and distinctions of all kinds. He was a knight of several orders, holder of many titles and diplomas. Many extraordinary distinctions were offered to him which he declined. One instance is very interesting.

At the announcement of Tesla's high frequency discoveries, while the former Emperor of Germany was all powerful and great men were eager for his favors, Tesla received an invitation from him and the Empress to repeat his celebrated experiments at the Royal Palace in Berlin. He forgot all about it and did not answer for one year, when he politely apologized for his inability to avail himself of the honour. Later the invitation was renewed and nearly two years passed before Tesla answered to the same effect. After a lapse of time, however, upon the announcement of another important invention, he received the invitation for the third time, with the assurance that an altogether unusual honour was reserved for him. "Well, boys," said Tesla to his assistants after he laid the invitation aside (and which he never answered), "the Emperor must be a great man. I do not think that I would be capable of acting in this way if I were in his place."

Perhaps the most remarkable tribute was paid to him when he made his famous experiments in Colorado in 1899. It was by J. Pierpont Morgan, the elder, who donated $150,000.00 which enabled Tesla to produce artificial lightning and incidentally, to electrify the entire earth. Some of Tesla's inventions were of far-reaching importance in the two world wars.

The resources and productive powers of the entire world, were greatly increased through extended use of his system of alternating current transmission and transformation of energy. Millions of horsepower of water falls have been harnessed by this means, thus saving a large output of coal and oil. The railroads have been completely revolutionized by the use of his ideas, such as the induction motor and electrical inventions of many kinds. His ideas also revolutionized the steel industry and operation of factories. Without going too deeply into the matter, it can be said with truth that without his inventions, we would have no electric light or power, no long distance telephones, no radios or television, no moon rockets, no radar, no motor cars, no dishwashers, no electric heat, no remote controls of any kind, no electric organs. There are many others, but with those few, the world would be back a hundred years.

The following is only a partial list of terms adopted and published in honest text books and technical works. I say honest because, in recent years the name of Tesla has been left out. However one has only to consult the patent office, to know that they are all Tesla's inventions.

    Tesla two-phase, three-phase, multi-phase, poly-phase systems of power
        transmission.
    Tesla principle, Tesla rotating magnetic field
    Tesla rotating magnetic field transformer
    Tesla induction motor, Tesla split-phase motor
    Tesla system of distribution
    Tesla rotary transformer, Tesla system of transformation by condenser
        discharges, Tesla coil, Tesla oscillation transformer.
    Tesla electrical oscillator, Tesla mechanical oscillator.
    Tesla high frequency machines, Tesla dynamo-electric oscillator.
    Tesla tube, Tesla lamp, Tesla high-potential methods.
    Tesla inductor, Tesla marvels, Tesla impedence phenomena
    Tesla electro-therapy, Tesla electrical massage, Tesla currents,
    Tesla transmission, Tesla experiments, Tesla capacity,
    Tesla arc light system, Tesla third brush regulation,
    Tesla devices, Tesla sparks, Tesla arrangements, Tesla theory,
    Tesla point, Tesla steam turbine, Tesla gas turbine,
    Tesla water Turbine, Tesla pump, Tesla compressor, Tesla igniter,
    Tesla condensors, Tesla electro-static field, Tesla effects,
    Tesla radio-systems, Tesla methods of wireless transmission of energy,
    Tesla magnifying transmitter, Tesla telautomata, Tesla insulation,
    Tesla underground transmission, etc., etc.

In all, there are 1,200 original inventions, which cover the entire world of this age.

-----0-----

On one occasion, Tesla was presented with a medal, -- a symbol of gratitude, together with a paraphrase of Pope's lines on Newton:

    "Nature and Nature's laws lay hid in night
    God said, 'Let Tesla be,' and all was light."

This was the man who said he was a Venusian, the superman who perhaps arrived on a space ship, the X-12, as a tiny baby, or again perhaps he came as a "thought," and he grew to maturity to fulfill his great mission, to set up the machinery for the new scientific civilization that will, some time in the future, lift the Aquarian Age to heights of glory. Two thousand years earlier Joseph watched over the Babe Jesus, while the Star of Bethelehem hovered above the stable.

Few people on this planet today have any conception of the herculean accomplishments of Tesla on behalf of the whole world.  But, no doubt, on other planets in this solar system and in systems beyond, the people are well aware that they can extend the hand of friendship to us now, in this new age, because of the mighty works of Tesla.

No doubt there are many earth people who will feel, even now, that Tesla would have found a way to overcome the obstacles placed in his path by the forces of darkness; that he should have forced a showdown that would have thrust his inventions upon the world, regardless of the ignorance and ambitions of a petty minded opposition.  But like the spaceman that he was, Tesla knew that he could only encourage us.  He could not force his light upon us. He could only respect our free will.  He was aware that humanity was palgued by the forces of darkness.  He well knew that people were unable to see the significance of his role as a Lightbearer.  He was never bitter, never disappointed, when people failed to appreciate his efforts.  He would only smile his slow, sweet smile in response to sympathetic friends who felt they must offer apologies for human arrogance and then he would quote in answer a favorite stanze from Goethe's Faust:

"The God that in my bosom lives
Can move my deepest inmost soul.
Power to all my thoughts he gives
But outside he has no control."

Well did Tesla know that each and every individual must find his own Christ-center, must contact his own Source.  For the doctrine of vicarious atonement is a vicious one, an escapist's dream.  Each must transmit his own misqualified energy; each must carve out and travel the razor-edged Path to the One God. Tesla's inventions can make the journey easier, as can the inventions of other great thinkers, if they are based on Truth.  But only God can say to each pilgrim on the Path, "Here is my gift.  Accept it, or reject it; learn by your past mistakes; then come home to Me."

There are those who will dispute the advantages of Tesla's inventions and the present developments made by Matthews and others who follow in Tesla's footsteps, arguing that machinery has nothing to do with discipleship.  There are those who will say that we must not use a mechanistic approach, such as the anti-war machine, in trying to solve our problems; that we must use only Love and understanding.  But this attitude stems from the dreadful devoteeism generated under the mis-used understanding of the truth as tuaght by Jesus.

Jesus was a practical man who lived in the workaday world.  He made His Ascension by the application of the Truth, which is the true scientific principle; which is the only method anyone can use.  It is the impractical mystic who views science as a handicap.  It is quite true that if men and women of good will could generate a sufficient amount of love and understanding, we could change the course of history at once, but the change would come about scientifically, for the energies generated in this way are simply collected by Angelic forces acting as accumulators and then poured into certain specified areas of atomic matter, freeing them from low vibrations and raising their frequencies so they can function with greater freedom.  There is nothing mystical in the process.  There is nothing mystical about an angel.  When angels walked and talked with men, they were accepted and not thought of as mystical, but as real and necessary messengers from the Divine Being.  They are not any more mystical than trees, rocks, soil, or rivers.  They are not one whit more mystical than the pigeons in the park.  It is the dark forces who have conjured up that phoney mystical story, so that people would feel that they had to be practical in the materialistic meaning of the world, and depend upon a job, a boss, a national ruler, a military machine, instead of simply depending upon God, His Son, and His angels.

So let us not despise a mechanistic approach which will allow us to lay down our weapons and give us the leisure time to develop the educated heart of love, the enlightened mind of Understanding. As the space people have quoted, "Do not count the teeth of a camel which has been given to you with love, but ride it with thanks in your hearts that you have a vehicle which will carry you safely through the hazards of the desert." Remember too, that Tesla's anti-war machine is simply a mechanistic version of the wall of light; it does not pretend to replace the supreme power of God. But God is not a dictator. He does not force His will upon mankind. We are free to make mistakes and if we are wise, we must learn by our mistakes. A good master never follows his workers around, telling them what to do and what not to do. On the other hand, a bad master does nothing else. Not trusting himself, he has no real love or trust for others. This kind is a coward and he even enlists the aid of teachers, doctors, newspapers and many other means, to assist him in his nefarious practice of enslaving the human mind through dictatorship. This kind of tyranny exists in virtually every part of the world today, and it is a well-known fact that the forces of darkness are especially proud of the inroads they have made in destroying family love and harmony. Divine Love does not direct His disciples to follow certain lines of thought, or point out to them certain ideas which they must absorb. The disciple must at all times use his or her discrimination, within the limits set by Divine Law and must through his own efforts learn to handle only that type of energy which will increase his working knowledge of Divine powers; and how to apply such power, by allowing himself to be used as a lens, through which God shines His power, by means of the cosmic ray.

Over the years many disciples have been sufficiently alert to apply ideas which they learned from Tesla, for disciples range far and wide in their search for truth, striving to recognize it and greeting it with joy when they find it. The mystic or the devotee usually makes the mistake of searching for truth only in nice but innocuous books, respectable surroundings, and sanctimonious environments. Therefore, it has not occurred to many persons to look into the findings of an electrical scientist like Tesla to confirm the Truths put forward by Christ. Tesla's scientific knowledge was four-dimensional. He believed in the spiritual nature of the universe and acted on the principle that all is governed by immutable law; that intelligence is present at every point in so-called space and can be acted upon through the power of thought. He astounded the scientific world by saying, in the year 1934, that a wall of light, invisible and impregnable, could be built around a nation. Its power to withstand any impact would be greater than that of any physical substance known to man, he said. Tesla was using thought dynamically to establish this wall of light from out of the very atmosphere in which we live, move and have our being. He called this invisible substance intelligent energy which could be thought into existence. He knew that thought was creative. "Building this wall was not a supernatural feat, for we were dealing with energy. I had already learned to draw this wall of light around myself, therefore it was not an impossibility to conceive of a wall of light around our home. Everybody has an atmosphere, or electrical field, and the atmosphere in which we live is filled with invisible atoms. The center of these atoms is the intelligence which keeps the electrons revolving around it like the planets around the sun, in an orderly fashion, according to law. The pattern of the atoms changes with changing thoughts. With the above understanding, we visualize the wall of light around our homes and their environs. We conceive of the outer surface as sending forth charges of electrical energy which will act as a repellant and result in completely discouraging all unwanted things,—including sickness, accident or thieves, negative thoughts of ourselves and others. Such things may come as far as the place where you visualize and accept the wall of light, but no evil regardless of its nature will enter. Now, during the present days which approach the end, all persons could rebuild this wall, or tube of light, for it will banish disease, death and disharmony without cost. In these last days, as the axis of the earth is changing and as the vibratory action on the planet is rapidly increased, it would indeed be the part of wisdom to seriously construct and use the tube of light. Each individual should use it, not for himself, but for others. It is usually not wise to inform the person who is being assisted, but we must not enforce our help on persons who do not want it. We must at all times do our best to help others without thought of receiving thanks. In fact it is the golden rule of silence. People could halt half of the trouble in the world today if they would just stop chattering like monkeys in a tree and listen to the Voice of the Silence that speaks from the depths of each beating heart."

In addition to using the wall of light around your country, town, or yourself, it would indeed be wise for every mother and father to keep the wall of light constantly around their children. But if it serves as a protection device only, most people will feel that this is assuredly a sufficient reward. This is a mistake, for in dealing with God's law it is extremely unwise to place any limitation on it.

That gambling attitude of, "Well, I'll take a chance, what have I to lose, maybe it will work and if it does I'm that much ahead," - is an attitude that might well carry one through a day or evening at Las Vegas, but in building the tube of light, one should begin by making an affirmation that is free from limitation. "I place a wall of light around myself that keeps me invisible, invincible and invulnerable to everything that is unlike Christ" is a free avowal. But it must not be left high and dry on the mental plane, for there it will prove sterile. Remember that most of the people who feel sorry for themselves are, for the most part, intellectuals.

It is their lack of feeling which prevents them from expressing any love for Christ. Therefore, when thinking of the tube, or wall of light into manifestation, it is necessary to feel very deeply about the glory of serving God.

There must be no feeling of personal glory, but rather a feeling that one is being absorbed, body and mind, back into the glory of God of which we are a part, according to His will. I know this sounds very religious, but there is no other way which I can find to explain this power, man has tried every other means under the sun, and has always failed, I refer to God's power in a very matter of fact way. After all, there should be no mystery about the power of God, why fool ourselves? Why blind ourselves to the fact that there is no power but of God: The wall of light is formed of electronic substance which is the primal life substance released from the great Power. How, or why this is, no man can know. There is nothing mystical or mysterious about it, for it is strictly scientific, as practical and demonstrable as the multiplication tables. Of course, the individual, in his heart, must know that God is the only sustaining power in the universe, otherwise he can not build the wall of light. In other words, one must be in tune with Divine Will; that is the only cost. The tube of light which you build around yourself will take on the quality of your own thought. Therefore, if you are in tune with God, if you believe, His protection is invincible, and an invulnerable protection, it will be just as you believe, no more or less. If you doubt in the least, in that case the wall will not exist because you have destroyed its power by your own distrust. It's all a matter of believing. The first step, therefore, is to know that God does exist, that He loves all people, and that He does have the power to command the electronic substance to surround you and remain permanently invulnerable to all that is not of the light. The process of manifesting the wall or tube of light is simple. It requires no money, no special equipment, no college degrees. It does, however, require a certain amount of practice, for one must be in tune with Divine Being. As with all true prayer, one must be undisturbed and without the least doubt, doubt is the one great thing which will prevent the manifesting of the wall of light.

Two or more persons should be able to be in tune with each other, and with God. For when two or more are gathered together in His name, He is right there with you. Then focus your attention upon your own Inner-Self, the Divine Presence within your own beating heart. If you are in tune, with the Divine, you will visualize a great tube, or wall, of invisible electronic light gathering about you, or, and, your nation. There is no limit to the bounds of its protection. Think great, and it will be as you think; never limit the power of God. The power of man, depending on his own limited power, is not great, but when we build the wall of light, it is not us, we are only the instrument used by Divine Power.

To be effective, we must be willing; and to be willing we must believe, otherwise there will be no good results. It was perfect faith, knowing the power of God, which enabled Joshua to destroy the walls of Jericho, by the means of 'sound' - the power of 'thought' (read that story in the Bible, book of Joshua, Chapter 6). No doubt, some time in the future, when chaotic conditions have cleared, every child will be properly instructed in the true, and simple understanding of the power of God, instead of the sometimes foolish man-made religions, which hog-tie our spiritual progress, to say little of our material being. Meanwhile, of course, every effort should be made to cease misqualifying the pure thoughts, or the reflection of Divine Power, as it leaves your heart. In other words, refrain from getting mad at yourself and the world around you, leave off all worry, cast out all fear. If your favorite worrying subject is lack of money, then use the thinking power that is wasted in worry in realizing that all supply is created by the Creator.

This forms a magnetic focus for supply and it will flow in naturally; but remember that doubt will immediately cause loss of power. God knows your every need, and if the need is worth while - from the Divine point of view - more than the need will be supplied. Christ said we do not receive an answer (supply) because we ask wrongly, cultivate an abiding faith in God, not simply because you want something, but from pure love, and you will find your outer world swinging into a wonderful new orbit of harmony. Remember that if you need special help at any instant of the day or night to solve any problem, you should call on the power of god. You will get an immediate response, even though you may not recognize the energy form in which it comes to you.

And when you gaze at the skies overhead on a clear night and see an apparent star shoot suddenly through the heavens, know that it might be a flight of cherubim speeding forth on some cosmic errand, would there be any harm to think we recognize them? Acknowledge, and bless them, and believe we will recieve their blessing in return. In the near future, more and more of these vehicles will become visible in the skies. Remember that at present all space ships and space people can use the tube of light at any time to make themselves invisible. As earth people themselves learn to form and use the wall of light, they will develop a consciousness which will make them fit companions for space visitors.

END

ADDENDUM

From the Files of Arthur H. Matthews

We Can See Without Eyes.  Answer to Will Irwin.

I know nothing about clairvoyance, fortune telling, or any similar foolishness, but I have received positive proof that telepathy is possible, under the
right conditions.  Telepathy as I understand it is very different to the ord-
inary dreams which may be the result of a disordered stomach or brain, but two
minds can be trained to be in tune with each other, and the training consists
chiefly in absolute concentration on each other, and love for each other.  In
fact great love between the persons regardless of sex is the principle require-
ment.  I do not believe a public demonstration could be made because any disturbing faction would distract the attention of one or other of the subjects.
The wife and I practiced telepathy years ago, and although we could not do
tricks, such as naming cards or similar things, we could however recognize a
'call.'  We would sit for hours on end in separate rooms, the understanding
was to concentrate.  She was to call me first using the simple word 'help' and
to think only on the thought "I want you," or the opposite call "O.K." and the
thought "all is well' and repeating the thought over and over again at the same
time visualizing the one the thought is meant for.  We would take alternate days
in the sending position, until we were able to recognize the correct call, at
any time, and after several months we could both do so.  We then extended our
mind "wireless" as we termed it to my job two miles from home. She was to call
me any time between 10 A.M. and 4 P.M., and I confirmed my call by calling her
on the phone.  This went on for some years, until one day, I had left home as
usual and had just arrived at work when I received the call "help" - as it was
only 8 A.M. I was inclined to doubt my senses but as the call continued, I phoned
and was astonished to hear the distressed voice of my wife telling me the stove
water jacket had "burst" and the water was flooding the kitchen!  Since this
occurrence we have both had occasion to use our "mind wireless" many times,
distance has no apparent effect on it, although we have had no occasion to be
apart any great distance.  We have kept in contact up to one hundred miles.  I
can prove one demonstration.  It occurred on "Major H" Camp located in the Lake
St. John Woods, about one hundred miles north of Quebec City.  It was just after
supper when I received the "Help" call.  I turned to the "Major" and told him
that I had a feeling that all was not well at home, and that I was making
"tracks" at once to catch the 2 A.M. train to town.  He said I was all wet but
made no objections to my going, so with one guide we set out for the station -
a nine mile hike and canoe ride.  We made the trail all right, and during the
trip to town I sent the "O.K." call.  Arriving, I found the wife waiting at the
station for me!  The baby had the first tooth and my brother who I had not seen
for twenty-six years had arrived.  And so we had further proof of this wonderful
thing - Telepathy.  It may be very difficult for some people to believe this,
but there will be many thousands who will try it and they will succeed if they
have enough patience and love for each other.  Otherwise it is a waste of time,
at least I think so.

A. H. Matthews.

R.C. Valadez
1168 Ayala Dr.
Apt. #4
Sunnyvale, Calif. U.S.A
94086

A.H. Matthews, E.E. Bsc.
Lac Beauport. Box 7 & 98
Quebec, Canada

June 22, 1971

Dear Mr. Matthews:

I recently received a letter from Mr. Nick Basura of Los Angeles,
California, and enclosed in his letter was a copy of your letter
to him dated May 24, 1971. I found your letter most intriguing.
But before I state why I am writing you, perhaps I should tell you
something about myself.

When I was a teen-ager I became quite interested in electronics
and during my studies I came across an article on how to construct
a Tesla coil, also included in the article was a brief biography
of Tesla. The article aroused my curiosity to find out more about
Tesla. I found the more I read about Tesla, the more intrigued I
became. It was during this time that I came across Mrs. Storm's
book Return of the Dove, where I read about you. I naturally
wanted to correspond with you about Tesla, so I wrote to Mrs. Storm
to try to obtain your address, but I received no reply. Time passed and I thought that I would never be able to contact you. However when I received Mr. Basura's letter I became overjoyed that
he had your address and had corresponded with you.

Upon reading your letter to him I was glad to see that you have
written a book about the great genius Nikola Tesla, and I hope
that you do find a publisher, because I would very much like to
read your book, for I think that Tesla was a fantastic individual.
I am also very interested in the inteplanetary transmitter-receiver
you have constructed based on Tesla's work in that area.

You mentioned in your letter to Mr. Basura that you also new the
late Wilbert Smith. Is that the same Wilbert Smith who was the
head of Canada's Project Magnet? If so, are you interested in anti-
gravity?

I hope that you will answer my letter, because I feel that you do
have undisclosed knowledge of Tesla and perhaps of other subjects
that is not only of great interest to me, but to others as well.

Sincerly,

Raymond C Valadez

Raymond C. Valadez

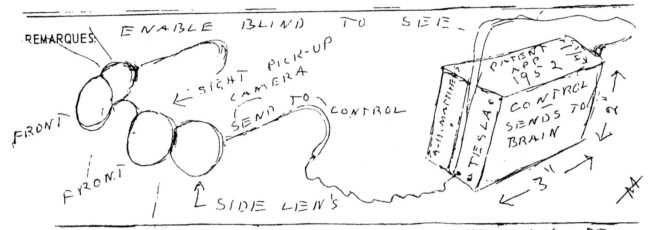

Labels within the figure:

REMARQUES.

ENABLE BLIND TO SEE.

←SIGHT PICK-UP CAMERA

SEND TO CONTROL

FRONT

FRONT

←SIDE LIEN'S

PATENT APP. 1952

CONTROL SENDS TO BRAIN

TESLA

3"

ANY NUMBER OF PICK-UP LENS CAN BE MOUNTED ON CONTROL- <u>WITHOUT USE OF EYE-GLASS</u>. NO LEAD-WIRES —OR PHYSICAL CONTACT · ARE REQUIRED.

Arthur H. Matthews

Ⓒ

MINISTER OF NATIONAL DEFENCE FOR AIR

OTTAWA, 25th June, 1940.

Dear Mr. Matthews,-

     The Minister has asked me to acknowledge with thanks your letter of the 19th June. So many inventions and suggestions have been received by this Department that it has been necessary to organize a special Board at the National Research Council to review them and report to the Department as to their best utilization. Your letter has been referred to this Board who will give it prompt and careful attention and communicate with you in the near future.

     It is suggested that all further communications concerning this or other suggestions be addressed directly to:-

> The Secretary,
> Inventions Board,
> National Research Council,
> Sussex Street,
> Ottawa, Canada.

     Also I desire to express my appreciation of your patriotic interest in forwarding your suggestion.

Yours sincerely,

James A. Sharpe,
Minister's Secretary.

*Please return to* Mr. A. H. Matthews,
Lake Beauport,
Quebec, P. Q.

3-6

COMMUNICATIONS SHOULD BE ADDRESSED
THE "COMMISSIONER OF PATENTS"
"OTTAWA"
WHEN WRITING ON THIS SUBJECT REFER TO
SERIAL NUMBER OF APPLICATION

CANADA

PATENT OFFICE

OTTAWA, February 26, 1944

| | |
|---|---|
| *Applicant* | A. H. Matthews |
| *Title of invention* | Methods for the Control of Insect Pests |
| *Filing date* | Feb. 8, 1944 |
| *Serial number* | 510,626 |

Sir:

You are hereby advised of the filing of the above application for patent.

Your obedient servant,

J T Mitchell
Commissioner.

To A. H. Matthews, Esq.,
Lake Beauport,
Que.

CIRCULAR No. 1
10 000—16-8-43

PLEASE RETURN MY COST,

CABLE ADDRESS " RESEARCH"

IN YOUR REPLY PLEASE QUOTE
FILE No. . 13-T-119

### NATIONAL RESEARCH COUNCIL
#### CANADA

OTTAWA, 1 August, 1940

A. H. Matthews, Esq.,
Lake Beauport,
Quebec, P.Q.

Subject:   Defence by Tesla currents.

Dear Sir:

Your letter on the above subject
dated   12 July, 1940
and addressed to   National Research Council
has been sent to the Inventions Board for consideration
and reply.

It is desired to inform you that after careful consideration the Examining Committee is unable to
recommend the use of your proposal.

Your desire to help in Canada's war effort
is greatly appreciated.

Yours very truly,

DC                     Examining Committee of the Inventions Board.

P.S.  Mr. Tesla has offered his death-ray invention to
      Canada some time ago and a detailed investigation
      has been made on that occasion.

PUBLISHER OF
RAILWAY AGE
RAILWAY MECHANICAL ENGINEER
RAILWAY ENGINEERING AND MAINTENANCE
RAILWAY ELECTRICAL ENGINEER
RAILWAY SIGNALING
MARINE ENGINEERING AND SHIPPING AGE
THE BOILER MAKER

PUBLISHER OF
LOCOMOTIVE CYCLOPEDIA
CAR BUILDERS CYCLOPEDIA
RAILWAY ENGINEERING AND
MAINTENANCE CYCLOPEDIA
BOOKS ON TRANSPORTATION

# RAILWAY
# ELECTRICAL ENGINEER

## SIMMONS-BOARDMAN PUBLISHING COMPANY

"THE HOUSE OF TRANSPORTATION"

NEW YORK
30 CHURCH STREET

CHICAGO
105 WEST ADAMS ST

CLEVELAND
50 PUBLIC SQUARE

WASHINGTON
17TH AND H STS N W

SAN FRANCISC
58 MAIN STREE

ADDRESS REPLY TO
30 CHURCH STREET
NEW YORK

January 24, 1935

Mr. A. H. Matthews
46 De La Ronde
Quebec, Que. Canada

Dear Mr. Matthews:

My secretary suggests you will probably spend this eight
bucks for a new wash boiler or some kind of electrical
equipment you don't need!   Of course that is no affair of
mine - but I want to disclaim any responsibility.

This check is offered in payment for your article "The Junk
Heap Super Phone", which was published in our January issue
and an extra copy of which is contained in the attached
envelope.

Yours very truly

A. G. Oehler, EDITOR

AGO:BR

THIS REFERS TO TESLA TRANSMITT.
RECEIVER BUILT BY ME AT 'SANFOR
125 MILES NORTH OF QUEBEC CITY.
A TESLA MICRO-WAVE-WHICH WAS
ABLE TO CONTACT NEW YORK CITY- 19

Members  Audit Bureau of Circulations and Associated Business Papers, Inc

# A National Weekly Newspaper Owned and Edited by the Railroad Workers of America

# *LABOR*

NOT PUBLISHED FOR PROFIT

ACCEPTS NO ADVERTISING

LABOR BUILDING 10 INDEPENDENCE AVENUE
WASHINGTON, D C
February 7, 1938

EDWARD KEATING, *Manager*
W P. NEVILLE, *Treasurer*

Mr. A. H. Matthews,
Lake Beauport,
Quebec, Que., Canada

My dear Mr. Matthews:

Please accept my sincere thanks for the information contained in your letter of February 4. If possible, we will give Tesla's suggestion a little publicity. We certainly need something to head off wars, and make it possible for little nations to defend themselves against the big nations.

Sincerely,

Manager

Ottawa, February 15, 1944.

Dear Mr. Lacroix,

I have your letter of February 10th with enclosures from Mr. A. H. Matthews, Lake Beauport, P.Q., relative to his invention for the improvement in methods for the control of insect pests.

I understand from the Commissioner of Patents that Mr. Matthews filed application for a Patent on February 8th, 1944. The Commissioner further advises me that his application is being dealt with without any undue delay.

I am, according to your request, returning the enclosures from Mr. Matthews.

Sincerely yours,

Wilfrid Lacroix, Esq., M.P.,
House of Commons,
OTTAWA.

THIS REFERS TO MY INVENTION OF SELECTIVE CONTROL- AT A DISTANCE - WITH NO PHYSICAL CONTAC- TO CONTROL ANY FORM OF GERM- ANY SICKNESS- ALL KINDS OF INSECT WHICH CAUSE DAMAGE- TO FOREST- GARDEN- AND -HUMAN.

135

JAMES McCUTCHEON & CO.
ESTABLISHED 1852
609 FIFTH AVENUE
NEW YORK 17 N.Y.
TELEPHONE
ELDORADO 5-1000

WILLIAM E. SPEERS, PRESIDENT & TREAS.
WALLACE C. SPEERS, VICE PRESIDENT
CHANDLER GUDLIPP, VICE PRESIDENT
JOHN O. McCUTCHEON, SECRETARY

SUBURBAN STORES
—
WHITE PLAINS N.Y
EAST ORANGE, N.J
MANHASSET, N.Y

September 18, 1952

Mr. Arthur Matthews,
Lake Beauport,
P. Q. Canada.

Dear Mr. Matthews:-

Thank you for your fine letter of September 9th.  I have been delayed in answering it because I have been away filling some speaking engagements.

I am happy indeed that you thought so well of our little article in the Peader's Digest.  You might be interested in what has been happening to it since it was published.

The reaction to it was enormous.  It gave me the chance to try out an idea.  I call it "spiritual commandos" - having people spotted all over the country who have a practical knowledge and experience in the spiritual approach to real problems like strikes, community tensions or personal difficulties - people whom you could send to places where problems arose.

Most of the letters we have received are from people in some kind of trouble.  Lacking money to help I wrote to people, some friends, some strangers saying "As a result of the article we have received the enclosed letter.  This person seems to be having more than his fair share of trouble.  I can't ask you to be responsible.  But sometimes just a friendly pat on the back and someone to talk things over with is enormously helpful.  Do you think you can do something to help this person?"

Perfectly splendid things have happened.  People in jail have been called on and helped.  People out of work have been found jobs.  Sick and crippled people have been aided - all because the human soul was touched and reacted from a warm heart.  It is one of the most hopeful and inspiring experience it has been my good fortune to be connected with.  It makes one think of the good Lord's statement

"Inasmuch as ye have done it unto the least of these my little ones ye have done it unto me."

Even at a time when strife and discord seem to be overwhelming the world, there still are wonderful things that people are doing for each other. Indeed they seem to be tickled to death to be given the opportunity. I believe that is enormously significant.

Again many thanks for your fine letter.

All the best to you.

Very sincerely yours,

Wallace C. Speers, Chairman
The Laymen's Movement for a
Christian World

(I am a member since it started -)

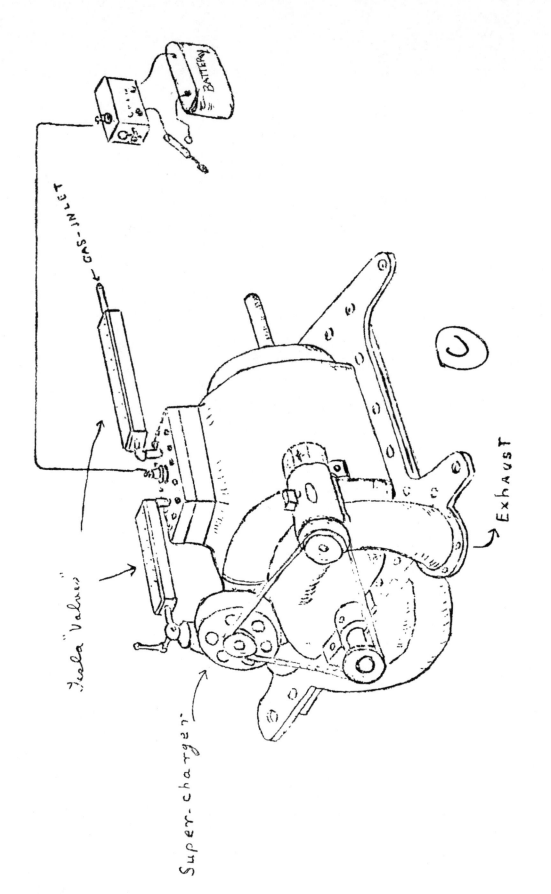

GAS - INLET

Battery

Scala "Valves"

Super-charger

Exhaust

C

Gasoline - Turbine - unit -

A. H. Matthews

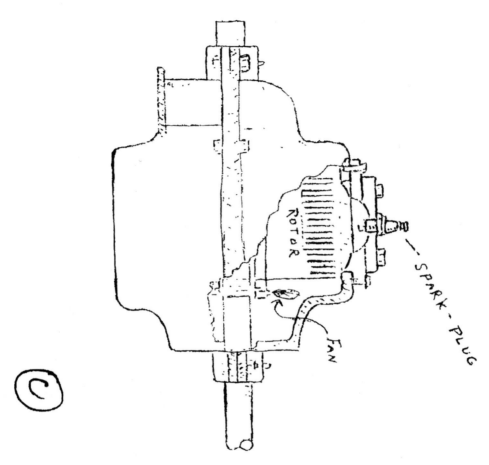

ROTOR

SPARK-PLUG

FAN

Tesla - Valvular - Conduit

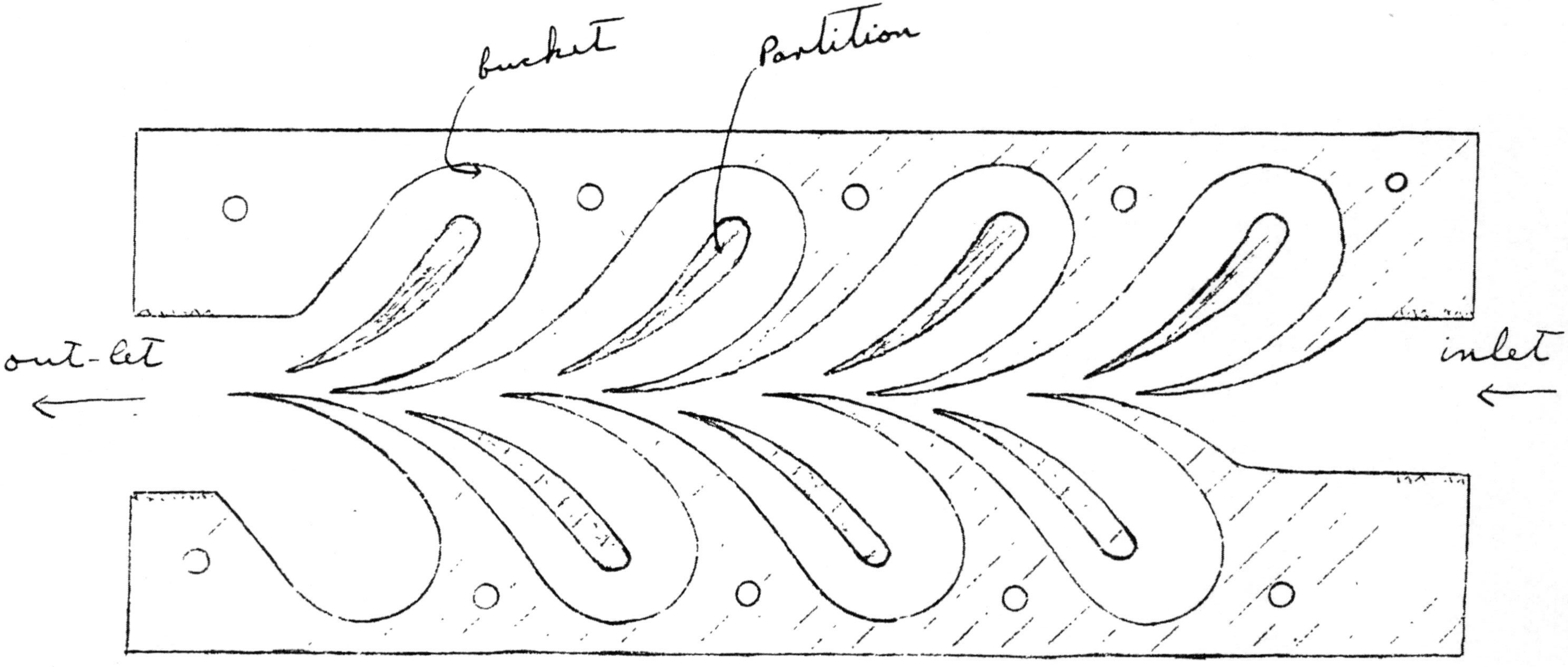

inlet

Partition

bucket

out-let

©

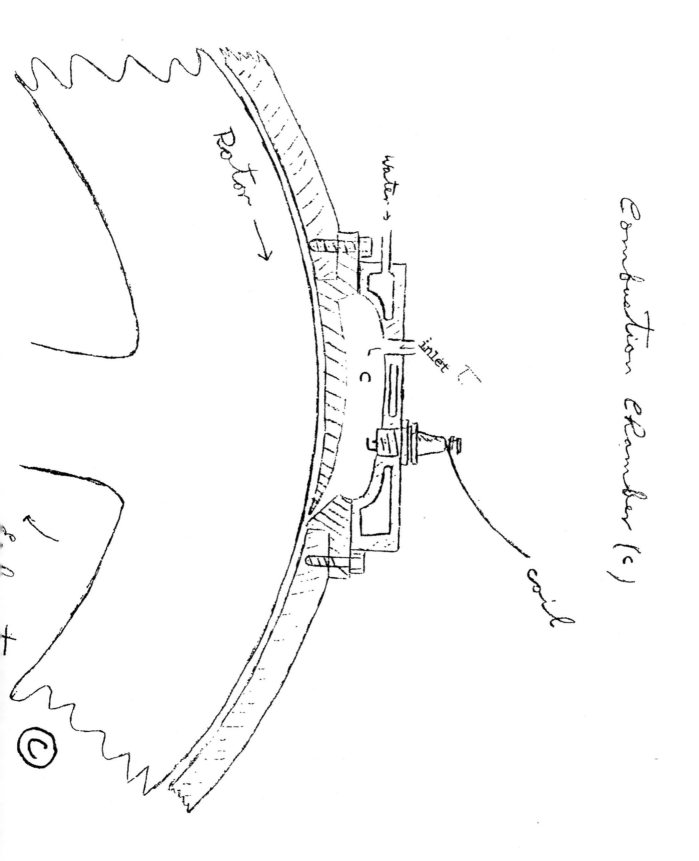

Rotor

water →

inlet

Combustion chamber (c)

coil

141

A. H. Matthews
Box 7. Lac Beauport
P.Q. G0A 2C0

Feb. 22, 1977

Dear Health Research:

Enclosed a few news clippings.  Sorry the one I sent was only a copy.  It was sent to me by a reader of The Wall of Light.

Andrew Michrowski - mentioned in news - received all of his first information about Tesla, from reading my book.  He came to see me early last year.  He works for the Sect. of State (Canada).

Since my book was published, I have received letters from all over.  I sent you a few some time ago.

A number of persons have come to see me from many countries - and wonderful news - almost every large paper in the world contacted me by phone during the past six weeks.  Some kept me on the phone over an hour.  Also, CBS, CBM, T.V. and Radio interviewed me, and the wonder is -- the T.V. gang were in my home 4 days last week.  They are going to put the story on world wide T.V.  The operators were from New York and Washington, D.C.  They took many still pictures of my 26 oil paintings (which are mentioned in The Wall of Light).  They are also on colour T.V.  My 26 pages of notes concerning the pictures were read into the T.V.  These pictures contain the keys to the secret of building the Tesla Wireless Transmitter of Electrical Power.  The news hounds say "Theory" but it is not a Theory, it is a practical fact.  I helped to build it three times, and can do it again.

I was invited several times to attend the meetings at Ottawa, which were held in the Federal Government Buildings at Ottawa,  To the best of my knowledge, I am the only one alive who knows how to build the Tesla Weather Control, and Wireless Power Transmitter, and perhaps the Anti War idea.

The method can be found in my book, The Tesla Patents & Lectures - so watch out for this T. V.  I will let you know the date.

The story was mentioned on T.V. last week and several times on the radio.  There is a great new interest in Tesla since "Return of the Dove" and The Wall of Light" were published.  A number of robbers have re-printed parts of both books - which helped to spread the news.

I will do as you suggest, try to get an original copy of the paper.  It was Stephen Aug who phoned me from Washington, so I will write to him.  I can use any number of ads you can spare.  I'm getting up to 20 letters a day, and I enclose an ad in my reply to them.

**HEALTH RESEARCH**

Best wishes.

(s) Arthur Matthews

# RADIO WAVES & LIFE

## There is strong evidence that life (human and otherwise) may be able to detect (or be affected by) radio waves.

### By TOM JASKI

IN a recent editorial (August, 1959), Hugo Gernsback called for a serious reappraisal of the effects of radio waves on human and animal physiology. In view of the almost casual use of high-power radar and industrial rf heating equipment, this is certainly a timely word of warning.

It is not surprising then that the Air Force is already keenly aware of these problems, and has a number of projects under way to discover the exact effects of high-intensity radar pulses and microwaves on human and animal tissue. These projects are being carried out at our major universities, each specializing in one particular frequency. For example, the project at the university of California, under the direction of Prof. Charles Süsskind, is primarily investigating the effects of 3-cm radar energy. Test subjects are mice, ants, and yeast cells.

### Thermal effects

Of great importance, and therefore under intensive investigation, are the thermal effects of such waves, and these have been measured rather precisely under a variety of conditions.

Using mice as subjects, it was found that near-lethal doses of radiation do not seem to cause any pathological changes in them, and that the lethal effect is primarily an overtaxing of the mice's temperature-balancing system. It was found that the major heating effect took place immediately under the skin, but of course heat generated there is rapidly distributed through the body. The temperature of the mice was monitored continuously. The photograph shows zoologist Susan Prausnitz monitoring the temperature of a mouse suspended in the wire cage right in front of the waveguide just visible on the left. The mouse is slowly rotated to insure even radiation over the entire body. Death occurred in 50% of the mice when a critical temperature of 44.1°C was reached.

Other interesting findings include the fact that radar waves appear to have no significant effect on the fertility of the male mice. The effects of radar waves on the longevity of the mice are currently being investigated.

An intensive series of experiments was carried out on cellular organisms, such as yeast cells, but, other than showing thermal effects, the experiments were inconclusive. Similar experiments with insects such as ants delivered relatively minor data. But one interesting item which emerged was that the ants, normally moving every which way, in a Petri dish, *will all line up in a 3-cm field, aligning their antennas parallel to the field,* apparently to minimize the effects.

The project is continuing, and more research on mice, ants and other animals is contemplated. Psychological effects will be looked into. One promising item in the ant experiments was that the ants which were exposed to 3-cm waves apparently lost the ability, at least temporarily, to communicate the source of food to their fellows, as ants usually do. It may be significant that the large ants used have antennas which measure very nearly one-fourth the wavelength of the 3-cm radiation.

Incidentally, mice are so frequently used for this kind of experiment because they are easily handled, easily obtained and relatively inexpensive, while their physiology and metabolism bear a useful resemblance to human counterparts in some ways. The life span of a mouse is limited, permitting experimenters to evaluate genetic effects over several generations.

Meanwhile other service branches are carrying out research programs concerned with the effects of radio waves on animal life, not necessarily limited to radar frequencies. A public announcement by scientists at the National Institute for Neurological Diseases concerning the lethal effects of 388-mc radio waves on monkeys also shows there is great interest in other frequencies and effects besides thermal.

### Some early reports

As long ago as 1930, Nrunori claims

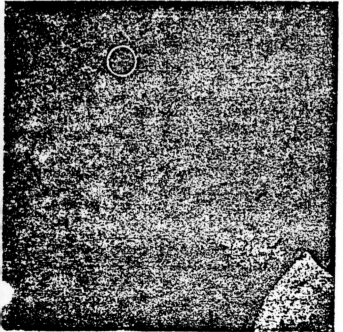

Zoologist checks the temperature of a mouse (circled object suspended in front of waveguide).

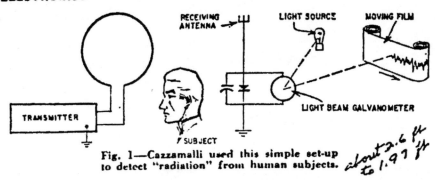

Fig. 1—Cazzamalli used this simple set-up to detect "radiation" from human subjects. *about 2.6 ft to 1.97 ft*

to have seen evidence that the human organism "radiates" and "reacts to" radio waves of 2.33 meters and its harmonics—in other words: 129, 258, 387 and 596 mc.

This brings to mind the work of a man who started publishing articles on this kind of subject more than 35 years ago. An Italian university professor named Cazzamalli placed human subjects in a shielded room, subjected them to high-frequency radio waves, and claimed to be able to record a "beat" which he received on a simple untuned receiver consisting of a galena crystal, a small capacitor, antenna and sensitive galvanometer. Cazzamalli's equipment, as well as it can be determined from his early articles, is shown in Fig. 1. The one item which he never mentions, perhaps because he could not accurately determine it, is the power of his transmitter. He published oscillograms purportedly showing variations of the "beats" when his subjects were emotionally aroused or engaged in creative efforts. Later experiments delivered much more startling results: he found that some of his subjects would hallucinate under the influence of high-frequency radio waves, which by then ranged all the way up to 300 mc.

The Cazzamalli experiments were carefully duplicated with modern equipment, of much greater sensitivity than his. His "oscillatori telegrafica" (presumably a transmitter as used for wireless telegraphy) was replaced with a very modest low-power oscillator. The reason for this was twofold. In the first place, university authorities take a very dim view of experiments on human beings, even if these subjects are the scientists themselves, volunteering for the part. Second, a previous experiment had indicated in a rather startling way that power was not required to evoke effects in the human nervous system. In fact, there seemed to be some sort of resonant frequency applicable to each individual human.

## Effects on humans

That experiment was suggested by the behavior of the monkeys we cited. These animals went through a sequence of behavior which would indicate that something besides thermal effects was operating. To discover if this "something" was subjectively noticeable by an individual, a weak oscillator was swept through the band from 300 to 600 mc with the request that the subject

indicate any points at which he might notice anything unusual. The subjects were not allowed to see the dial. At a particular frequency, varying between 380 and 500 mc for different subjects, they repeatedly indicated a point with almost unbelievable accuracy (as many as 14 out of 15 times).

Subsequent experiments with the same subjects showed that at the "individual" frequency, strange things were felt. Asked to describe the experience, all subjects agreed there was a definite "pulsing" in the brain, ringing in the ears and a desire to put their teeth into the nearest experimenter. The oscillator in this case was putting out only milliwatts of power, and was placed several feet from the subject.

## Optical and growth effects

It was not the first time that such phenomena had been observed. Van Everdingen, a Dutch scientist, had discovered many years ago that radiation would affect the heartbeat of chicken embryos, when he was experimenting with the effects of high-frequency radiation on growth (specifically working toward any effect it might have on malignant growths). Van Everdingen used 1,875 mc and 3,000 mc and discovered that this kind of radiation would change the optical properties of a glycogen solution. Glycogen is a substance which occurs very abundantly in chicken embryos, particularly at an early stage of development. It is also the substance which provides our muscles with energy! Van Everdingen found that this change of optical polarization had some connection with tumor growth. He proceeded to re-rotate the polarization in extracts obtained from tumor-producing mice. When this optically "pure" substance was injected into mice with malignant tumors, *and these mice were kept on a diet free of animal fats, the tumors would cease to grow.* Only radiation at uhf or shf would produce these effects in the substances he used.

But Van Everdingen was not the only one who discovered important facts about radiation on living tissues. Years before, a Frenchman named Lakhovsky claimed to have removed tumors from patients with high-frequency radiation treatments, and his book, *The Secret of Life*, has a number of attestations in it from grateful patients who were cured. Lakhovsky stated that healthy plant growth is materially aided by

placing a copper ring about 8 inches diameter and supported on an insulating wooden stick (Fig. 2) around the plant. So-called tumerous growths plants disappeared within such a ring Lakhovsky's experiment with plant has been duplicated successfully. B then we should also note that the sax kind of thing has been done by a grow of devout citizens using group praye

But the people who have publish the most data on the subject of u radiation effects on animals and hum subjects are the Russians. In *Biofisi* the Russian biophysics journal, a scie tist named Livshits published two sy vey articles on the work that had be done in this field by 1958 and 1959. Th are too extensive to repeat in great tail here, but some of the more impre sive highlights will be reported.

Many experiments were carried on animals with conditioned reflex and one by Glezer showed that a we uhf field would inhibit the condition reflex, indicating that some inhibiti of the cortex was taking place.

As in Van Everdingen's experime with chicken eggs, Pardzhanidze show that the EEG's of rabbits were dr tically changed when the animals we subjected to a uhf field. Bludo Kurilova and Tikhonova showed th the field produced an increase of sen tivity in the retina, and simultaneou reduced the area of color sensitivity. is interesting to speculate how t would correlate with the Land effec (Land, of Polaroid camera fame, h shown recently that our concepts three-color vision may well be fal and that color vision seems to depe primarily on the presence of two ima stimulated by two different frequenc of light!)

Turlygin similarly showed that sensitivity of the eyes of dark-adap subjects at marginal levels was creased as much as 100% by the pr ence of a uhf field.

## Nerve effects

Of importance in the light of L hovsky's claims is the experiment

Fig. 2—A copper ring, eight inches diameter, seems to improve plant gro (after photograph in *Secret of Life* Lakhovsky).

Made in United States
North Haven, CT
01 June 2023

37245367R00080